MISSOURI NORTH
The History of Lutheran Church–Canada

D1714081

© 2022 Lutheran Church–Canada
Reprint 2023.

LUTHERAN CHURCH–CANADA
ÉGLISE LUTHÉRIENNE du CANADA

3074 Portage Ave.

Winnipeg, MB R3K 0Y2

Telephone: 204-895-3433

FAX: 204-897-4319

© 2022 Lutheran Church–Canada.
Reprint 2023.

Scripture quotations are from the *ESV®* Bible (*The Holy Bible, English Standard Version®*), Copyright © 2001 by Crossway, a publishing ministry of Good News Publishers. Used by permission. All rights reserved.

We thank the Provincial Archives of Alberta, which houses the material of the Lutheran Historical Institute, Katie Lazure (Archivist), and Karen Baron (former Archivist), for their assistance with *Missouri North*.

TABLE OF CONTENTS

FOREWORD

I extend my thanks and gratitude to all who contributed to this book on the history of Lutheran Church–Canada: to one of our eminent church historians, Rev. Dr. Norman Threinen, for authoring the first nine chapters; to Rev. Dr. Edward Lehman, Rev. Dr. Ralph Mayan, and Rev. Dr. Robert Bugbee for their observations and recollections during the years they served in the office of Synod President, from the founding convention of LCC in 1988 until 2018; to Rev. Dr. David Somers for his record of LCC's French Ministry; and to Rev. Mark Lobitz, who served as editor.

Missouri North might seem a rather unusual title for a book about the history of Lutheran Church–Canada; yet it is most fitting and proper. This is especially borne out in a letter, dated February 11, 1856, from the founding father of the Missouri Synod, C. F. W. Walther, to an unidentified pastor here in Canada. Lutheran Church–Canada is currently transitioning into a new way of doing things what with the restructuring of our Synod, and all the unforeseen issues and details that have arisen as a result. Moreover, at the time of writing we are also in the midst of the COVID-19 pandemic and government restrictions on in-person worship services, which has resulted in great hardships to our pastors and congregations.

As a result, and in the brief time I have served as Synod President, it seems to me that Walther's words are even more timely and fitting for the pastors and members of the congregations of Lutheran

Church–Canada today than they were 165 years ago. Here are a few excerpts from Walther's letter that mirror my thoughts as you begin to read *Missouri North:*[1]

Dear brother in the faith,

Grace, mercy, and peace from God the Father and from the Lord Jesus Christ, the Son of the Father, in truth and in love.

I am very happy to see that also in the far north in your area the Lord is beginning to arouse souls and that the pure Gospel, as God permitted it to be preached again through His precious servant Luther, is finding a place there. May God bless and further these God-pleasing undertakings. For it is certain that anyone who thinks only about having a church, without also asking and inquiring whether the unfalsified Gospel will be preached therein, will only help in the building up of the tower of Babel which here in America is being constructed so eagerly by a hundred different sects. All sects come and go like comets, but the star of our true orthodox church of the Unaltered Augsburg Confession will continue to shine forth, even if the star here and there is clouded over somewhat. For 'God's Word and Luther's doctrine pure shall now and evermore endure.' As much as our small Lutheran Catechism is despised, yet it is a fortress that cannot be conquered no matter how much the world assails the Bible fortification. For in all other catechisms of the sects there are all kinds of rationalistic propositions, yet in the treasury of our precious catechism there is nothing but pure gold. May God strengthen you to raise up high the pennant of our church there so that all the misled children of our church may again be gathered under this banner and many others also be attracted into the one faith

---

1   From the *Selected Writings of C.F.W. Walther: Selected Letters*, tr. Roy Suelflow. Concordia Publishing House, 1981: 67-69.

confessed in one love and one hope.

Do not tire of planting the church of our pious fathers in your midst and do not fail to do what you can towards this purpose. For since this matter is most important and obviously displeasing to Satan, but pleasing only to God, therefore the flesh, the world, and the devil will thoroughly oppose it and will seek to weaken you in your undertaking and make you discouraged.

The enthusiasts and the religious syncretists have an easy go of it, for they yield here and there to the devil, the world, and the flesh. For such people to make a beginning in church work is therefore usually not very difficult. But they build on sand, and when the rainstorms come, the whole structure will collapse. The orthodox however have a difficult beginning, for they usually have only a few people, and sparse resources, and are despised by the proud children of the world and by the false saints. But pursue the right course, and your structure will stand firm, which no storm can blow down, because it is built on the rock, namely the rock of Jesus Christ and His eternal, pure, divine Word.

The Lord be with you and yours and all those in your church. Please greet everyone for me in a fraternal manner, those who love the Lord and love His undiluted Word.

Your friend and brother in the Lord,
C. F. W. Walther

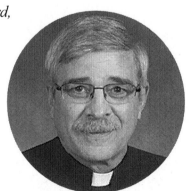

Rev. Timothy Teuscher, President
Lutheran Church–Canada
Winnipeg, Manitoba | May 2021

PART 1

MISSOURI NORTH

Rev. C. F. Walther, Director of Western Canadian Missions
for the Minnesota District of the Missouri Synod.

CHAPTER 1
Setting the Stage

In the decade between 1831-1840, thousands of immigrants from Europe crossed the Atlantic Ocean to the United States. Since many of them were Germans, Lutheranism in the United States experienced great numerical growth. In contrast to earlier waves of immigrants who were primarily attracted by the prospect of good farmland, many of those who arrived in the decade of the 1830s were shopkeepers, tradesmen, and industrial workers. Industrialization, which had taken a firm hold on the economic structures of Europe, had deprived many people of their livelihood. As a result, North America became the economic "promised land" for many.

In addition to those who sought a more secure life financially, some immigrants were motivated by religion. By the nineteenth century, the rationalism of the Enlightenment was so strongly entrenched among Protestant clergy, especially in Europe, that they generally dismissed traditional Protestant Christianity. Confronted by this trend and encouraged by the publication of a new edition of the Augsburg Confession in 1819 and the writings of Martin Luther in 1826, Lutherans in Germany experienced a confessional renewal.

Among the confessional Lutherans who emigrated to the United States for religious reasons were a group of seven hundred Lutherans from Saxony. They formed an emigration society in 1836 in hopes initially of establishing a theocratic community in America. The bulk of the community ultimately settled in Missouri and, under the influence of leaders such as C. F. W. Walther, attracted others to form the Lutheran Synod of Missouri, Ohio, and Other States.

Among the signatories of the new Synod was a young, former shoemaker named Adam Ernst. Although he had only received one year of theological training in his native Bavaria and had only limited knowledge about America, Ernst was instrumental in bringing together a meeting of the Saxon leaders which resulted in the formation of the Synod in 1847. And, six years later, in response to a "Macedonian Call" from a congregation of German Lutherans in Rainham Township, Canada West (modern day Ontario), he helped extend the Synod into Canada.

When German immigrants came in large numbers to the United States in the 1830s, many also came to Canada; the population of Canada West trebled in the twenty years after 1820, and German immigrants contributed to this growth. Some German settlements established Lutheran congregations with the help of missionaries from the Synods in New York State and Pennsylvania; these organized an indigenous Synod of Canada in 1861. Other settlements relied on vagabond clergymen who had arrived with the settlers. The congregation in Rainham Township—somewhat isolated off the north shore of Lake Erie—was one of the latter.

Adam Ernst in 1849 accepted the call to serve as the pastor of a congregation in Eden, New York near Buffalo. Since Buffalo attracted many of the recent German immigrants, Ernst's responsibilities included serving as a mission developer for the entire area. Recognizing that many German settlements lacked satisfactory pastoral care, the Missouri Synod decided to commission colporteurs, or distributors of religious tracts and books, to reach out to them with Bibles and other literature. One of these colporteurs was based in Buffalo and it was through his work that the Rainham congregation first learned about Ernst and invited him to visit. When the Middleton Township (modern day Rhineland, Ontario) further west learned of Ernst's visit, the congregation there also asked him to provide pastoral services. The Missouri Synod mission to Canada was born.

For the next year, Ernst served these congregations every four weeks as outposts of his Buffalo area congregation. In January 1855, the congregation in Middleton formally joined the Missouri Synod and installed its own pastor. A year later, the congregation in

Rainham did the same. After he had provided the two Canadian congregations with resident pastors, Ernst withdrew his involvement. But eight years later, while he was serving a congregation in Ohio, Ernst was called to a Missouri Synod congregation in Canada West, which was an outgrowth from the Rainham congregation. As a result, he became actively involved for the next sixteen years in the development of Missouri Synod congregations throughout the province.

Rev. Adam Ernst, first missionary pastor to serve Canada.

***

As was true of every other congregation, congregations in Canada West were automatically assigned to a District of the Synod—initially, the East and later the North District. They sent delegates to Synod and District conventions and exercised all the rights and responsibilities of synodical membership. When they were vacant, they could call pastors from elsewhere in the Synod, and Canadian pastors could accept calls to American congregations. If there were issues with which the Synod was dealing, they were affected like all other congregations in the Synod. On the other hand, their geographic location in Canada gave them an identity which was distinctly Canadian. The "governing authorities" which the Scriptures required them to pray for and obey (Romans 6) were Canadian, not American, authorities. They needed to obey different tax and property laws. They had a history which differed from their fellow Lutherans in the United States, and this affected their thinking in various ways.

To address matters unique to the Canadian congregations, they launched their own church paper in January 1871. Adam Ernst was a frequent contributor to it. In general, such articles served the same educational and inspirational purpose in Canada as the official church paper of the Synod. Since the pastors of the separate Canada Synod accused the Missouri Synod of being a foreign intruder in the country, such actions helped support the claim that the Missouri Synod had been properly called to serve in Canada. It also gave voice to the need to have a separate District in Canada.

As a first step toward a separate District in Canada, the Synod in 1873 formed a separate Canadian circuit with fourteen pastors serving a score of congregations. Adam Ernst was elected to head the circuit. In preparation for further development of a District, pastoral conferences were held in Canada. Finally, on April 17-23, 1879, a convention of pastors and congregational delegates was held at which the Canada District was born. Adam Ernst was elected as its first president. In his impromptu report, he acknowledged the need to form the separate District. "Congregations in Canada see themselves as politically and geographically separated from the [United] States," he said.[1] The official paper of the Missouri Synod also supported this development in Canada.

By forming a Canada District, the Missouri Synod did not spawn

---

1   *Proceedings*, The First Convention of the Canada District, 1879, 5.

a separate synod in Canada as the congregations of other Lutheran Synods had done. Canadian congregations and their pastors continued to remain members of the Missouri Synod in every way. Yet, the formation of a District did constitute the first steps in a process which would lead to the formation of a separate Canadian synod when the time was right.

***

While the Missouri Synod in Ontario was reaching greater maturity through the formation of a Canada District in 1879, developments were also underway which would bring the Missouri Synod into Western Canada. By that year the vast prairie region, which the British government had transferred to the newly confederated nation of Canada, was being surveyed to pave the way for settlers. At the same time, the Missouri Synod was working vigorously to reach German immigrants settling in the Minnesota and Dakota Territory of the United States. When the Synod created a Northwestern District, it seemed only natural that Manitoba and the entire Canadian prairie region would be included in this District.

Although pastors of the Synod made trips across the border into Canada, the 1880s saw little apparent progress in Western Canada. It was only in the last decade of the nineteenth century that ethnic German settlers began to arrive in large numbers. Some came from Ontario, others from the United States; but the greatest number of them came from Russia, the Austro-Hungarian Empire, and other parts of Eastern Europe. By this time, the Canadian Pacific Railway, with its spurs to the north and to the south, was also being built.

As the new frontiers continued to move toward the border from the south, the Missouri Synod continued to subdivide its Districts.

Throughout this development, however, Western Canada remained intact as the home mission territory of the Minnesota District. It was this District which sent both of the first resident missionaries to Western Canada—to Manitoba in 1891 and Alberta in 1894. As congregations developed in Western Canada over the following three decades, they became part of a single circuit of the Minnesota District, stretched out over a vast territory which was roughly 1,300 kms wide from east to west. Recognizing the difficulty of administering such a huge territory, Western Canada was subdivided into two circuits in 1909: one for Manitoba and Saskatchewan, and one for Alberta.

To oversee the development of the Western Canadian mission, the Mission Commission of the Minnesota District designated one of its members by the name of C. F. Walther. Although a contemporary wrote that Walther "dreamed, thought, talked, planned, and lived Canadian missions," he continued to reside in the United States. To give on-site attention to the work, the Commission called four provincial travelling missionaries. To help create more interest in the work in Western Canada, a church paper was launched by "the pastors of the Ev. Luth. Missouri of Western Canada" in January 1914. The paper provided a forum for discussing whether it was time to divide the Western Canadian region into one or two Districts.

To man the mission in Western Canada, the District looked to the steady supply of graduates from the Synod's seminaries. Although the congregations they served were part of the Minnesota District, the pastors were nevertheless aware they were serving in a foreign country. After two or three years, most of them were emotionally overwhelmed and physically exhausted by the constant travel expected of them and were happy to accept a call back to the United States. The frequent turn-over of graduates assigned to the Canadian mission field resulted in many Western Canadian congregations being slow to take responsibility for their own work.

Gradually, however, as some American-born pastors remained in Western Canada and made Canada their permanent home, the church in Western Canada eventually recognized that it was incongruous for the direction of the church to be determined by mission directors living in the United States. This realization eventually led to the separation of the Western Canada mission from the Minnesota District and the formation of two Canadian Districts in Western Canada in the early 1920s.

**

While there were now Canadian Districts in both Ontario and Western Canada, the Lutherans who made up the Missouri Synod in these two regions differed greatly from one another. Most of the Synod's members in Ontario had immigrated to Canada from their homeland in northern Germany or from the Eastern United States where they had experienced a mature, settled church life with church buildings and pastors. By the time settlement was occurring in Western Canada, congregations in Ontario were well established with their own churchly traditions, including substantial church buildings to carry on ministry in their communities. They had a history of being part of the Missouri Synod almost from the beginning and had been mentored by pastors who were concerned about forming in them a solid doctrinal basis for their faith and church life.

In Western Canada, which had a sprinkling of adventurous immigrants from Ontario and the United States, congregations were overwhelmingly made up of immigrants from the various territories of the Austro-Hungarian or Russian Empire. Their German ancestors had left southern Germany in the middle of the eighteenth century and had lived for several generations in areas where trained pastors were scarce. The pastors they had were called upon to oversee and supervise numerous congregations in a larger region. The spiritual care of individual members was generally provided by lay preachers or by the heads of families in their homes. Religious instruction had been very basic and tended to be laced with Pietism so that their religious views were often hard to distinguish from Moravians and Baptists. Pietism was a faith emphasis which focused on the individual believer rather than the community of the faithful.

The Canada District developed before the Missouri Synod had developed a system of funding for home missions. It did not have a home missions committee in 1879. As a result of their past experiences, German Russians felt that pastors should be paid by the government. In Western Canada, because of the poverty of the immigrants, pastors were supported from the mission offerings of the Minnesota District as a whole. This led many immigrants from Eastern Europe to assume that in Canada the District was responsible for paying pastors, just as the governments had done in Europe.

Because Missouri Synod Lutheranism in Ontario generally had a strong theological basis, it tended to be more traditional. Developed largely in a frontier context, Lutheranism in Western Canada tended to take more practical approaches to issues and be more open to new directions to address local issues.

Additionally, Missouri Synod Lutherans in Ontario confronted just one German Lutheran Church body from which they were separated on the basis of history and theology. By contrast, the immigrants from Eastern Europe and Russia—who constituted the bulk of Missouri Synod Lutherans in Western Canada—were confronted upon arrival in the area by missionaries of several German Lutheran synods. In their eyes, all of them seemed to have much the same conservative theological orientation; conflicts among Lutheran groups appeared to be mostly a struggle for mission territory rather than genuine conflict over theological issues. As a result, congregational affiliation with a synod was often based on which synod could provide a pastor. Individual congregational affiliation, in which the immigrant had a choice, was decided based on where the immigrant had settled, what hymnal was being used, and on pastoral practice.

In Ontario, many congregations developed along with the Synod as a whole. If the Synod was experiencing theological conflicts internally or with another synod, these conflicts were also often experienced in local congregations. In Western Canada, the divisions which had resulted in the different synods predated the arrival of the immigrants. As a result, the divided Lutheran scene appeared to the immigrants to be an importation from the United States; it was something to be tolerated but was ultimately of little importance to these immigrants struggling to establish themselves on the Western Canadian frontier.

These differences in how Missouri Synod Lutheranism in the Eastern and Western part of the country developed had a marked impact on the later attitude of Lutherans toward their countrymen in other regions of Canada.

CHAPTER 2
In War and Peace

For several decades, these two faces of Canadian Lutheranism, east and west, subsisted basically independently of one another. They were both authentically part of the Missouri Synod; pastors were graduates of the same seminaries, and congregations from both regions looked south to St. Louis and synodical leadership there; District presidents and other church leaders had contact with one another at conventions and other church meetings. But on the local level, there was little contact between Canadian members in Missouri Synod congregations from different regions and little interest in what was occurring among their fellow Lutherans in other parts of the country.

International events would bring a change in attitude. As Canada was drawn into World War I, Missouri Synod Lutherans in both parts of the country were suddenly confronted with a common experience—the experience of being German in a country which was part of the British Empire and thus at war with their ancestral homeland. Although they still had little or no contact with one another, Lutherans in both parts of the country took steps to affirm their loyalty to Canada and the British Empire in the face of suspicions of disloyalty from the majority of the population in the country.

The demonization of Germans by the Canadian press and a predominantly English population was bound to be felt particularly in Ontario, since the province accounted for 43 percent of the country's enlistments in the armed forces in World War I. Because the Missouri Synod was viewed by the general population as German, the war retarded the development of new missions in the Ontario District and disrupted normal church life in many ways. To show its loyalty to Canada and the British Empire, the Canada District cancelled its 1916 convention and, in 1918, adopted a Loyalty Resolution in which it pledged "energetic and unswerving support to the limit of our capacity and ability." Although the Synod did not want the Church to get involved in politics, the District encouraged its membership "to render full and loyal service in those tasks which the Government has asked of them... as citizens... for the successful prosecution of the war."[2]

The war did not have the same extreme affects in Western Canada as it did in Ontario, but Missouri Synod Lutherans were also impacted there. In predominantly German rural communities, life generally went on as usual. But in the cities, promising mission work came to a stand-still. In Vancouver, the congregation had to be reorganized after the war. In Calgary, where several congregations had sprouted and grown, only one remained in 1918. In Edmonton, members were forced by loss of jobs to move into outlying rural communities. Particularly significant was the closure of German-speaking church schools as a result of war measures action in 1916.

Because the Synod did not as yet have a District structure in Western Canada through which Lutherans could speak to the government and defend themselves from public abuse, individual pastors showed their Canadian patriotism in other ways. In Wetaskiwin, south of Edmonton, local Missouri Synod pastors combined the celebration of the 50th anniversary of Canada's Confederation in 1917 along with the 400th anniversary of the Lutheran Reforma-

---

2   Threinen, *Like a Mustard Seed*, 67.

tion. Their celebration drew a crowd of 800 people, and included a large procession headed up by the Canadian flag. In Edmonton, pastors organized a German-Canadian Association and conducted mass meetings in different localities to discuss the hate propaganda of the war period, pressing for a fair and equitable treatment of all citizens. "O Canada" was translated into German for use in public meetings, and Sunday-School lessons and confirmation classes were conducted in English.

By 1914, C. F. Walther and Minnesota District officials had realized that the time was right to give District status to the Western Canadian prairie region. With Canada at war, however, the formation of a District was postponed; planning for a District in Western Canada from an American base would have encountered innumerable difficulties. Immediately after peace was proclaimed, however, the first steps to form a District were taken as pastors and lay delegates from Western Canada were excused from attending conventions of the Minnesota District to give them opportunity to plan for the formation of two Districts in Western Canada.

After a series of District-style conventions, the Alberta-British Columbia District was formed June 30, 1921, and the Manitoba and Saskatchewan District on July 13, 1922. While Missouri Synod Lutherans in Canada still did not have a formal apparatus which would enable them to work together, the two faces of Canadian Lutheranism at least had corresponding church structures which could relate to one another in a concrete way: the president of the Ontario District now had Western counterparts at meetings of District Presidents in St. Louis, and Synod Conventions had delegates from across the country representing their Districts. Finally, issues which were distinctively Canadian could, for the first time, be discussed and mutually dealt with by those who were church leaders in their country.

***

Two decades after the "war to end all wars," the world was once again engulfed in global conflict. Across Canada, the loyalty of Germans was again questioned. To remove any doubt about the loyalty of its members, in spite of its continuing public image as a German Church, the Ontario District in convention in 1940 passed a "Reaffirmation of Allegiance" and later forwarded a message of sympathy to the Royal Family at the news that the King's brother had been killed in active duty. Similar actions were taken by the two Districts in Western Canada and appeared prominently in church newspapers.

The war had the effect of moving many young people out of the protective environment of the rural communities in Western Canada where they had grown up. Irrespective of whether they had been raised in Ontario or in Western Canada, young men from Missouri Synod congregations across Canada volunteered for action. In addition, large numbers of young women migrated to the cities in Ontario and British Columbia to take jobs in war-related industries. Initially, church leaders assumed that contact with Missouri Synod young people who had entered the Canadian military would be maintained by the Synod's Army and Navy Commission office in the United States. However, sending their names and addresses to an agency in another country was against Canadian wartime regulations. On the prompting of concerned Canadians, as a result, the Missouri Synod appointed a three-man, Ottawa-based Army, Navy, and Air Force Advisory Board to maintain contact with military personnel. When this task overwhelmed the members of the Board, it was taken over by three volunteer District Service Boards and later by a Canadian office of the Synod's Army and Navy Commission in Winnipeg. This attention to the needs of its young people in the Canadian armed forces formally brought together Missouri Synod Lutherans across the country in a joint effort for the first time.

***

This ministry to young men in the armed forces had ramifications beyond its significance as the first joint Canadian venture by Missouri Synod Lutherans. It raised new questions about the implications of working with other Lutherans as well as other Christians. Prior to this time, the pastors and congregations in Canada, along with the rest of Synod, had tended to live largely in isolation from other Lutherans and other Christians; their efforts to guard against doctrinal impurity prompted them to remain aloof of activities involving altar and pulpit fellowship with churches with which they were not in doctrinal agreement. Even praying with other Christians was viewed as engaging in sinful fellowship. Some pastors had participated in free conferences on occasion but the majority had little or no interaction with those outside their own church circle. The involvement in wartime services led Missouri Synod Lutherans in Canada to realize that, if they were to play a role in the broader context of their nation, they needed to have a more positive relationship with other Lutherans and other Christians.

Thus, when a conference of Canadian representatives of the North American Lutheran bodies met to mobilize for the challenge of wartime service through the formation of the Canadian Lutheran Commission for War Service, representatives of the Missouri Synod attended as observers; they felt that formal participation in the Commission would violate their fellowship principles. The Canadian representatives of the Missouri Synod set up their own structure with an office in Winnipeg, but the Canadian government was not prepared to recognize more than one Lutheran agency. For this reason, the Synod's Canadian director worked closely and amicably with fellow Lutherans for much of the war through the pan-Lutheran Commission.

Working with other Lutherans and other Christians to accommodate government regulations was relatively easy. But Missouri Synod chaplains in the armed forces who attempted to carry out a ministry to armed forces personnel with theological integrity faced greater difficulties. The Regulations of the Canadian Chaplaincy Service clearly held that Lutheran chaplains were "Protestant" chaplains and were to serve all Protestants—even when it came to providing the Lord's Supper. To address this issue, the Missouri Synod's Army and Navy Commission took the position, which also applied in Canada, that those non-Lutherans who desired to partake of communion celebrated by a Missouri Synod chaplain constituted "a separate and individual case." Those who came for communion need only recognize the importance of repentance and accept the Lord's Supper as a means of Grace.

Rev. Harold Merklinger, pastor, military chaplain, and advocate for increased autonomy for the Missouri Synod districts in Canada.

CHAPTER 3
Toward Autonomy

As the war in Europe continued, Missouri Synod pastors and congregations in Canada were called upon to relate more and more to the world outside their own small circle. In the process, they began to realize that the public image of the Missouri Synod in Canada as a German church based in the United States made outreach to Canadians difficult. The Missouri Synod had already dropped the word "German" from its official name at the time of World War I. Years later it would consider another change to its name in the face of World War II. This led some church leaders in Canada to wonder whether perhaps the time had come for the Synod in Canada to adopt a name which would identify it as Canadian. This issue was discussed at a joint pastoral conference of the two Missouri Synod Districts in Western Canada in Edmonton in 1941.

Among the participants of the Edmonton conference who supported the name-change was a young, Ontario-born pastor, Harold Merklinger. The community where he had grown up had witnessed a name change from Berlin to Kitchener during World War I. His own feelings of Canadian nationalism had increased during the years he had studied for the ministry in St. Louis, Missouri. Upon graduation in 1938, he had been sent to serve a new mission in North Vancouver—a sign that the Missouri Synod was beginning to recognize that its Canadian Districts had a common identity which was unique across the country.

One of the pastors whom Merklinger met at the conference and grew to appreciate was a prominent Saskatchewan pastor by the name of Christian T. Wetzstein. Although he had been born and raised in the United States, he spent thirty-two years doing ministry in Western Canada as a developer of new congregations in the District. He had also served as the president of that District for three years. During his ministry, Wetzstein had quite naturally become aware that community members often resisted joining congregations of the Missouri Synod in Canada because they did not regard it as a Canadian church. He had also come to recognize the importance of the unity of the Missouri Synod in Canada, as would become evident in subsequent years.

The members of the joint western conference agreed that it would help the spread of the Gospel in Canada if their church was identified as Canadian. To give a focus to this issue, Merklinger and Wetzstein brought to the conference a resolution requesting that the three Canadian Districts form a corporate body with a name which identified it as Canadian. The conference, in turn, asked the three Canadian Districts to consider this matter at their next conventions and appointed a committee, including Wetzstein and Merklinger, to carry out the resolution.

The western District presidents were cool to the issue, however, and none of them brought the conference resolution to their convention. Within the Ontario District, the idea was studied by the Eastern Pastoral Conference and rejected. The conference declared: "We do not believe that the name 'Missouri Synod' is dangerous to our prestige at all just now.... [It] is a good name because many people realize that the name has something to do with the United States of America and friends of the British Empire, including Canada."[3]

The concern for a more Canadian identity appeared to die when Merklinger joined the Canadian army as a chaplain in 1942. He was posted overseas and spent most of the war serving with the armed forces in Europe. As a result, he did not pursue the issue of a Canadian name for the Missouri Synod in Canada for the duration of the war. But while he was overseas, he became aware that two Lutheran congregations in the City of London, England and congregations in other parts of Great Britain were moving toward forming an autonomous Lutheran Church in England. In 1954, the Evangelical Church

---

3   Quoted in Schwermann, *The Beginnings of Lutheran Church–Canada*, 8.

of England came into being, with the Canadian-born Rev. E. George Pierce as its first president.

***

On his return to Canada in 1945, Merklinger picked up the idea once more. He addressed a letter to the three Canadian District Presidents and drew their attention to the 1941 conference resolution. He noted that various international businesses incorporate their Canadian Industrial branches under Canadian names. "If business firms see the necessity of having a national name to gather in dollars and cents, why should we not do the same thing to gather in immortal souls?" he wrote. Merklinger pointed out that the Lutheran synod in Australia had a distinctly national name. The Evangelical Lutheran Church of Brazil and the Evangelical Lutheran Church of Argentina also identify with the countries where they were located. "If Lutherans in other parts of the world see value in identifying with their country, why should Canadians not do the same?" he asked.

Merklinger's first letter received no response from the District Presidents, but the flurry of post-war activities and subsequent changes drew their attention to an emerging new world. Representatives of the Canadian units of the American-based National Lutheran Council churches met to form a corresponding Council in Canada and invited the Missouri Synod in Canada to become part of it. To determine whether and under what circumstances the Missouri Synod in Canada might be involved in it, the District Presidents and others who would later play a prominent role in the beginnings of Lutheran Church–Canada met with their counterparts in the other Lutheran bodies and amongst themselves for discussion.

One area of cooperation was the participation of the Missouri

Rev. Traugott O. F. Herzer worked with Lutheran Immigrant Society in Winnipeg which later became CLWR, and served as a liaison to the Canadian Government for Missouri Lutherans.

Synod in the formation of Canadian Lutheran World Relief (CLWR), which showed that the Synod was shifting its position on fellowship with other Lutherans. Where the Synod had previously remained aloof of all cooperation, it was now willing to cooperate in externals, such as providing physical relief for the millions of displaced German refugees in Europe. Based on this openness of the Synod to cooperate in externals, T. O. F. Herzer, a former Missouri Synod pastor working for the Canadian Pacific Railway at the time, and Richard Meinzen, the director of the Missouri Synod's wartime services office in Winnipeg, became major players in the creation of CLWR, which assisted refugees with food and clothing and brought many of them to Canada and a new life.

This new openness also filtered down to the Canadian Districts of the Synod. Each District named representatives to serve on the Board of Directors of this inter-Lutheran organization. Used clothing was collected in depots in several Canadian cities and then channelled to a parallel organization in Hamburg, Germany for distribution to those in need. Horace Erdman, the Executive Secretary of the Ontario District, was given a leave of absence and sent to Europe for a number of months to serve as the Director of the Canadian Christian Council for the Resettlement of Refugees, an inter-denominational relief agency. Thus, as the Missouri Synod in Canada came into a working relationship with other Lutherans, it was drawn into a relationship with other Christian bodies, as well.

As they participated in these external activities, Missouri Synod leaders in Canada also grew in their desire to seek closer relationships with one another. In July 1946, Ontario District President Frank Malinsky travelled to a high-level meeting in Edmonton which looked at ways and means of establishing closer relationships between Ontario and the two Western Districts.[4] Following the meeting, Erdman, who accompanied Malinsky to the meeting, travelled about in Western Canada, taking pictures to produce a slide lecture to familiarize people in Ontario with Western Canada.

***

Since Merklinger had not received any response to his earlier letter, he sent a follow-up letter to the District Presidents in 1949. In it, he not only reminded them of his earlier correspondence, but also proposed the idea of forming an entirely autonomous Canadian church or synod as the Australian Lutherans had done. If anyone hesitated on account of finances, he suggested that "as long as we adhere to the Scriptural principles of our Synod, we shall merit their [the Synod's] financial support. The mother synod supports work among other synods, and I am sure [it] would not forsake its work here in Canada."[5]

All three Districts now had new leadership and the new District

---

4   Threinen, *Like a Mustard Seed*, 144-146.
5   Cited in Schwermann, *The Beginnings of Lutheran Church–Canada*, 10.

Presidents were more open to Merklinger's proposals.[6] Each of them appointed a three-man committee with the directive that they meet with their counterparts in the other Districts to study the formation of a corporate body. As a result, on April 4-5, 1956, ten Missouri Synod men (nine pastors and one layman) met at the Marlborough Hotel in Winnipeg. It was the first meeting of representatives of the three Districts specifically to discuss giving the Missouri Synod in Canada a name which would identify it as a Canadian Church.

The joint committee agreed that incorporation of the three Districts as a Canadian body would help identify the Missouri Synod in Canada as a distinctly Canadian body in its contact with the government and the public. The members of the joint committee also hoped that with a Canadian name it would awaken members of the Synod in Canada to their unique mission to fellow Canadians. Finally, incorporation with a Canadian identity would facilitate the development of a self-governing Lutheran Church in Canada.

***

Significantly, along with the representatives of the three Canadian Districts, the joint committee included a representative of the non-geographic English District of the Synod. The District had no congregations in Western Canada, but it had become present in Ontario in 1921 when St. John's Lutheran Church in Toronto transferred to it from the Ontario District, thereby bringing to Canada's largest city insights into the "how" of urban ministry. Thirty-three years later, an English District congregation had also sprung up in Niagara Falls. St. John's had further planted three additional English

---

6   Serving as District Presidents at the time were Carl Basse, 1951-60 (Alberta-British Columbia), Leonard Koehler, 1951-70 (Manitoba and Saskatchewan), and Walter Rathke, 1948-60 (Ontario).

District congregations in the Greater Toronto area. As immigration to Canada increased after World War II, St. John's had played a significant role in assisting new immigrants physically and spiritually, and it was felt that involvement of an English District representative would be of benefit for the development of any future Lutheran Church in Canada.

Without a dissenting vote, the joint committee recommended the incorporation of the three Districts as a national body. Two subcommittees were created to advance this goal: one chaired by Albert H. Schwermann, recently retired from the presidency of Concordia College in Edmonton, to draft a constitution; and another chaired by Horace H. Erdman, the Executive Secretary of the Ontario District, to draw up a charter.

***

In August 1958, the three Canadian District Presidents jointly issued a notice authorizing the calling of a convention to form The Lutheran Church in Canada. The organizing convention met in Winnipeg on September 11-12, 1958. Nineteen men were present, including the three District presidents and three visitors. Arne Kristo, who had attended the previous meeting as a representative of the English District, was again present, along with a layman from a Toronto area English District congregation. The convention devoted most of its time to adopting a proposed constitution which Schwermann's committee had drafted. After it had been approved, a Board of Directors was elected.

Well-known after thirty-seven years at the helm of Concordia College, Schwermann was elected president of the new entity and its Board of Directors. He had served his entire ministry in the

Rev. Horace Erdman, who drafted the charter for the Lutheran Church–Canada Federation (LCC F).

Rev. Dr. Albert Schwermann, first president of LCC F, elected in 1958.

Alberta-British Columbia District but his position as President of Concordia College had involved him repeatedly in the affairs of the Missouri Synod. During World War II, he had also met with Canadian war-time officials to plead for an exemption from the draft for ministerial students. He had a broad knowledge of the Canadian Church, especially in Western Canada.

The other officers on the new organization's Board of Directors were: Arne Kristo, vice-president; Maynard Pollex, a former World War II army chaplain, serving as the pastor of an Ontario District congregation in Hamilton, secretary; Clare Kuhnke, a layman from Winnipeg, treasurer; and David Appelt, a layman from Saskatoon, member-at-large.

Since the whole venture dating back to 1941 had come about

Travelling to LCC F's Founding Convention in 1958:
Rev. Carl Baase, William Fromson, and Rev. Albert Schwermann.

largely as a concern for better public relations in the broad sense, one of the first Boards created by the Board of Directors was the Board of Public Relations. Appropriately, the members of this Board were from English District congregations in Toronto: George Bornemann, Arne Kristo, and Jack Ansett.

Erdman's committee was directed to proceed with incorporation and with securing a charter for the organization. The corporation was approved by the Senate of Canada on April 23, 1959, receiving royal assent the same year on June 4.

***

As its president, Schwermann served as spokesman for the new Lutheran Church–Canada. In his report to the 1958 conventions of the three Canadian Districts and to the Missouri Synod in San Francisco in

1959, he emphasized that Lutheran Church–Canada was not a church or a synod in the accepted sense of the term. It was a "federation" of the Canadian Districts of the Missouri Synod—a concept not generally used within Missouri Synod circles. It was a legally incorporated entity through which the Missouri Synod in Canada could speak with authority in dealing with federal and provincial governments as well as with other church bodies. The federation was intended to project an image to people, both inside and outside the church, that the Missouri Synod in Canada was a Canadian entity.

To calm the fears of those who might see the formation of Lutheran Church–Canada as a fracturing of the fellowship between the Missouri Synod in Canada and its mother church in the United States, Schwermann pointed out that it left unchanged the relationship which pastors and congregations had with the Missouri Synod and its Canadian Districts. For those who were disappointed that this new entity was not an autonomous Lutheran Church in Canada, there was the promise that the federation which constituted Lutheran Church–Canada would study the matter of autonomy and lay the groundwork for the "eventual" formation of an independent Canadian synod.

Because it was a federation of Districts, parishes were not represented at its annual conventions in the same way they were represented at conventions of the Synod or its Districts. Instead, each of the three geographic Canadian Districts was represented by only four delegates: two pastors and two laymen; and the nongeographic Districts were represented as a group with two delegates: a pastor and a layman.

***

Although studying the possible formation of an independent Lutheran Church in Canada was only listed as the fourth purpose of Lutheran Church–Canada in its constitution, this direction quickly became the focus. The Board of Directors created various kinds of Boards and named individuals to them. Reports from Canadian Lutheran World Relief and the Canadian Armed Services were brought to conventions.

To identify what would be required to operate an independent Church in Canada, the Board engaged in a fact-finding process from October 1959 to May 1960. This was followed by a summit meeting which brought together leaders from the Missouri Synod and their counterparts in the Canadian Districts. The summit identified a number of "aspects peculiar to the Canadian scene," including "the arrival of [post-War] new Canadians; an unrealistically large percentage of population claiming church affiliation; urbanization; far-northern developments; ethnic groups; etc"— leading delegates to the 1960 convention to conclude that "the proposed Lutheran Church–Canada must recognize and meet the need of a Canada-wide home mission strategy and have an aggressive evangelism program."[7]

The move toward creating an independent Church in Canada was applauded by Lutheran Church leaders in other countries. Among them was the president of the Lutheran Church in Brazil, which had been a recipient of Canadian candidates in the 1930s. He wrote to Schwermann, "I wish God's blessing on your endeavour. It will be a step forward. The more quickly a Church stands on its own national feet, the better it is for the Kingdom of God.

---

7   Cited in Schwermann, 50. One might specifically add French Canada to the list.

Our experience has shown how blessed it is when native-born men are given leadership positions and are made responsible. It causes the entire Church to become aware of its responsibilities."[8]

Determined to organize an independent Synod as early as possible, the delegates to Lutheran Church–Canada's 1960 convention resolved to have an organizational structure and other necessary recommendations prepared for the 1961 District conventions and for the 1962 convention of the Missouri Synod in Cleveland. They were subsequently shared in detail with the three District conventions in 1961 and approved.

The delegates to the 1960 Lutheran Church–Canada convention recognized that if the Districts were to approve the structure and other recommendations relating to their plans, the rank and file of the membership throughout Canada would need to know about them. Thus, a Board for Internal Information and Promotion came into being. Since Schwermann had become the recognized face of Lutheran Church–Canada to the Missouri Synod constituency in Canada, it was crucial that he continue to spearhead its promotion and became a member of this committee.

But Schwermann was already sixty-nine years of age and was finding that his duties as president, combined with teaching a full load of courses at Concordia College, were too much for him to handle. He needed to reduce his workload. To do so, the Board of Lutheran Church–Canada asked Concordia College to grant Schwermann a sabbatical leave which would permit him to serve as president full-time for a year. During this sabbatical year, he would devote all his attention to promoting a vision of an inde-

---

8   Cited in German in Schwermann, 26, footnote 5. Translation by the author.

pendent Lutheran Church–Canada. Schwermann's sabbatical extended from August 1, 1960 to August 1, 1961. For an entire year, he conducted seminars throughout Canada, publicizing Lutheran Church–Canada. Travelling by plane, train, bus, and car, he attended pastoral conferences and spoke to individual congregations. Special attention was given to Ontario and isolated areas in various parts of the country.

At its fourth annual convention from May 23-25, 1961, Lutheran Church–Canada was still basically on track, except the delegates realized that the original schedule had to be adjusted to allow time for congregations to vote on the issue. A complete progress report would still be given to the three District conventions in 1961 and to the Missouri Synod convention in 1962, with a congregational vote on the establishment of an independent Lutheran Church–Canada to take place in the first six months of 1964. As soon as the approval of two-thirds of all the congregations in Canada was received—provided it included a majority of the congregations in each Canadian District[9]—steps would be taken to form an independent Lutheran Church in Canada. If there was sufficient support from the congregations, the Missouri Synod would then be asked to give final approval in 1965.

Although a progress report had been prepared to be shared with the Districts in 1961, some issues had not yet been settled. One of them related to Canadian congregations which were members of non-geographical Missouri Synod Districts. The drafting committee had not envisioned that such congregations would form separate Districts in Canada; they would be encouraged to join Lutheran

---

9   Subsequently changed to two-thirds in each District by action of the Ontario District.

LCC F Executive Committee circa 1961. Back: Rev. Maynard Pollex, Clarence Kuhnke, Charles Opper QC. Front: Rev. Albert Schwermann, Rev. Fred Schole, Rev. Horace Erdman.

Church–Canada and be allocated to the geographical District in which they are situated. However, the Canadian Council of the English District had asked that in an autonomous Canadian Church, the English District congregations in Canada would become an English District of Lutheran Church–Canada. The overture to provide for this was declined by Lutheran Church–Canada, which strongly urged the congregations of the English District in Canada to seek admission into one of the geographical Districts instead.[10]

In addition to adjusting the schedule, new officers were elected at the annual convention in 1961. Schwermann was nominated as president but declined for health reasons. He was succeeded by Frederick Schole. Other officers were: Horace Erdman, vice-president; Maynard F. Pollex, secretary; Clarence Kuhnke, treasurer;

---

10   For the complete overture and response, see Schwermann, 58-61.

Rev. Fred Schole, second president of LCC F, elected.

and Charles Opper, an English District lawyer from Toronto, member-at-large.

Schole was well suited to succeed Schwermann as president of Lutheran Church–Canada. He had served with him on the Board for Internal Information and Promotion. He was a vice-president of the Alberta-British Columbia District and had held leadership positions in various Edmonton-area organizations. He had been elected to the Executive Committee of Canadian Lutheran World Relief where he subsequently served as President for thirteen years.

The progress report Schole sent to the Missouri Synod convention in Cleveland in 1962 provides a picture of what Lutheran Church–Canada would have looked like had it become a sister Synod of the Missouri Synod at that time. The Canadian church would have been self-governing and independent but would have required financial assistance from the Missouri Synod in many important areas: higher education, home missions, its church extension fund, foreign missions, and pensions. It would also have looked to the Missouri Synod for programming and training support provided by its various departments. In addition, it would have expected a free exchange of pastors, teachers, and full-time church workers between the two churches. In response to the report, the

Missouri Synod encouraged Lutheran Church–Canada to proceed with its plans for an indigenous church in Canada.

As the new year dawned on January 1, 1964, Missouri Synod Lutherans across Canada may have wondered whether that year would see Lutheran Church–Canada become independent or whether it would remain a federation of the Canadian Districts of the Missouri Synod. Philip Fiess, who had been elected President of the Ontario District in 1959, had argued persuasively that it would be a mistake to become independent—that the disadvantages clearly outweigh the advantages of moving in that direction. Leonard Koehler, long-time President of the Manitoba and Saskatchewan District, had strongly disagreed with him. In a last ditch effort to encourage congregations to vote in favour of independence, Harold Merklinger had written a compelling article in the December 1963 issue of *The Canadian Lutheran* entitled "How Shall I Vote?" "If we are to bring the Gospel to more and more Canadian citizens," he said, "we must do that as a Canadian church, Canadian in name and in fact."[11]

The vote by congregations on the issue was taken between January 1 and April 30, 1964. Ninety-four percent of all voting congregations in Canada exercised the franchise. Seventy-seven percent of them voted in favor of becoming an independent Lutheran Church. However, a two-thirds majority was needed in each District, and the vote in the Ontario District was below the required benchmark. The vote had failed.[12]

---

11 Harold Merklinger, "How Shall I Vote?" in Schwermann, 91.

12 Voting in favour of an independent Canadian church broke down as follows: Alberta-British Columbia (90.5 percent); Manitoba and Saskatchewan (85.4 percent); and Ontario (48.6 percent). Only half of the Ballots sent to English District congregations were returned. Of these, 75 percent voted in favour. See Schwermann, 98.

***

Despite the extraordinary efforts of Schwermann and the Board of Directors in promoting the formation of an independent Synod in Canada, more than half of the congregations in Ontario rejected the proposal. It is worth considering why. By 1964, the District had numerous individuals within its membership who could have assumed leadership roles in an independent church. Among them were a Member of Parliament and other politically-connected individuals; lawyers, teachers, architects, and other professionals; and university and similarly-trained people. A number of these individuals had served on boards of the Missouri Synod.

President Fiess put his finger on an important reason why congregations in Ontario voted against an independent Lutheran Church in Canada when he said: "It means cutting a great number of close ties."[13] For eighty-five years, the Ontario District had participated in the broader history of the Synod. It had not felt it necessary to recruit its own pastors; most of the pastors in the District, even in 1964, had been come from congregations in the United States. It had looked to the Synod to produce its educational literature. It was difficult to conceive of the Ontario District without its attachment to the Synod.

On a more personal level, people in Ontario had close ties with nearby American Districts. Pastors and lay people in the District felt a kinship with people in the New England states; they moved easily across the border to take part in events in the United States. They lived in a different country and they had a distinct identity, but Missouri Synod Lutherans in Ontario felt closer to their fellow

---

13   Ibid, 87.

Lutherans in the Eastern United States than they did to Lutherans in Western Canada with whom they had minimal contact historically. As they looked west, they felt things were just moving too quickly in the oil-rich and self-confident province of Alberta. They were much more comfortable with the stability which characterized their lives in Ontario. To turn their backs on their history and to link up with fellow Lutherans in Western Canada whom they did not know or trust would be unnatural. It would call for a drastic change in their thinking of the Missouri Synod in Canada.

By contrast, what accounted for the overwhelming support for an independent Lutheran Church in the two Western Districts? The congregations in the west were generally of more recent origin. Most of the pioneers had departed the scene but their descendants continued largely to regard the divisions among Lutherans as an American transplant to the Canadian scene. As a result, the Church in the west had fewer emotional ties to the Synod as a whole than was true in Ontario. Many pastors had either grown up in the west and had their initial training at Concordia College in Edmonton, or had come as seminary graduates from the United States and become Canadians. By 1964, the Alberta-British Columbia District had elected its second native-born District President. Another factor was that the areas north and south along the international border were not heavily populated and the contact by Canadians with their fellow Missourians in the United States was limited.

Western Canada in general was a place where people looked to what was possible through cooperation. With their oil-fields and their increasingly-large farms, people looked to the future with optimism. The church there reflected this culture and tended to expect continued blessings in the future. The two prairie Districts also struggled with pastoral supply and with funds but they felt they could manage on their own if they needed to. President Leonard Koehler put it this way: "The easy way is to depend upon the mother church to supply us with men and money.... It takes faith, courage, and a spirit of sacrifice to build the Kingdom of God under any circumstances.... Where is there a church that has both enough men and enough money?"[14]

Schwermann and the other proponents of an independent Lutheran Church–Canada shared this Western Canadian mindset. They had difficulty understanding how Lutherans in Ontario thought about life and about the future. An independent Lutheran Church–Canada seemed only logical. It was part of growing up as Canadians. It was obvious to them that they should move toward independence.

A final factor affecting the vote in Western Canada was Concordia College, Edmonton. It is significant that the leading promoter of an autonomous Lutheran Church–Canada in the early 1960s was the man who had led Concordia as president for decades. Concordia College had been part of Schwermann's vision for the Church in Western Canada. Although a new president for the college had been named by this time, the vision which the college represented had largely been realized. For almost forty years, the Edmonton college had recruited theological students, providing the initial stage of their training and shaping them for the type of ministry which most of them would carry on in Western Canada. Although their concluding years of theological training were spent in a seminary of the Synod in the United States, those years in a foreign country only accentuated for most students

---

14   Leonard W. Koehler, "A Letter to the Editor", in Schwermann, 88.

that ministry in Canada was unique. It only encouraged the hope for an autonomous Lutheran Church in Canada in the future.

This vision of an independent Canadian Church was not one which was easily communicated to the Missouri Synod Lutherans in Ontario, despite the efforts of Schwermann. It simply was not part of their lives and experiences.

Concordia College Edmonton early 1920s.

CHAPTER 4
An Administrative Unit

F ollowing the vote in 1964, Lutheran Church–Canada remained a federation. As such, nothing in the life of the Missouri Synod in Canada was altered. The relationship between the Canadian Districts and the Synod continued unchanged. Each of the Districts continued to sent pastors and lay delegates to conventions of the Synod. Offerings flowed from the Districts to the Synod and financial subsidies continued to flow from the Synod back to the Districts. Each District President still represented the President of the Synod in his District.

However, the groundwork for the independent Lutheran Church had been laid. In anticipation of autonomy, the three Districts had set up joint national committees for home missions, university and college work, public relations, young people's work, relief and immigration, relations with other church bodies, boy scouts and girl guides, social welfare, and armed service commission under the charter of Lutheran Church–Canada. Although the Canadian Districts were not ready to become an independent church, the Synod and the Board of Directors of Lutheran Church–Canada felt that they could as a body still serve a useful purpose in promoting the work of the Kingdom if they became an administrative unit of the Missouri Synod with broader authority and new powers.

Without being specific as to the nature of the broader authority and new powers which might be given to Lutheran Church–

Canada[15], the latter petitioned the Synod to designate it as its national administrative unit in Canada. The constitutional relationship of the Districts, congregations, and pastors to the Synod continued unchanged, but the Synod would delegate to Lutheran Church–Canada specific areas of nation-wide work which would be authorized from time to time, in consultation with Lutheran Church–Canada and the approval of the Canadian Districts. As its administrative unit for Canada, the Synod would recognize the right of the Canadian Districts to operate as a unit within the charter of Lutheran Church–Canada in those areas of Kingdom activity where the three Districts agreed that the work of the Lord could be done better jointly than if it was done singly. Concerned about continuing the momentum under this new model, the 1964 Convention re-elected the same officers for Lutheran Church–Canada except that Carl Wagner, the financial manager of the Manitoba and Saskatchewan District, was elected treasurer.

The 1965 convention of the Missouri Synod approved the concept of Lutheran Church–Canada as an administrative unit of the Synod. After all three Districts had also approved it, Walter Wolbrecht, Executive Director of the Missouri Synod, officially informed President Schole: "The Board of Directors of The Lutheran Church—Missouri Synod herewith recognizes and establishes that the Lutheran Church–Canada has fully complied with Resolution 4—28 adopted in 1965 in Detroit and is now an Administrative Unit of the Synod." One would have expected that such action would have been acknowledged by a bylaw change in the Handbook of the

15   Examples of the "broader authority" and "new powers" which the administrative unit might have had in mind might have been those granted to the Lutheran Church in America – Canada Section: e.g., bringing overtures to a convention, consummating fellowship, merger, and so forth.

Synod. One would have expected that the relationship between the Synod and the Canadian Districts would have changed. But little or no changes occurred as a result of the new designation.

***

The only obvious area where Lutheran Church–Canada seemed able to serve as an administrative unit of the Synod in Canada was in the area of inter-church relationships. The 1960s had witnessed North American Lutheran Church mergers resulting in the formation of the American Lutheran Church in 1960 and of the Lutheran Church in America in 1962. With only two churches remaining, a Lutheran Council in the United States seemed unnecessary unless the Missouri Synod participated—an action toward which the Synod was now favourably inclined. On the basis of meetings with representatives of the National Lutheran Council, the Synod had concluded that agreement had been reached on the doctrine of the Gospel and subscription to the Lutheran Confessions. If there were issues where there was no consensus, the provision had been made for a Division of Theological Studies within the Council to discuss them. On this basis, the Synod approved membership in the Lutheran Council in the United States.

Because questions about the future need for a Council had also been asked on the Canadian scene, the answers in Canada were the same. A Council in Canada was therefore patterned after the one in the United States, and the Missouri Synod also approved membership in the proposed Lutheran Council in Canada. It was only natural that Lutheran Church–Canada would participate in its capacity as an administrative unit of the Synod in the proposed Lutheran Council in Canada. It was specifically to address issues which might arise in the Canadian context that the Canadian Lutheran Council was formed. If the Missouri Synod constituency in Canada was not yet ready to put its energies into becoming a separate church body, it could nevertheless be put to use in a cooperative setting with other Lutherans.

In anticipation of the participation of the Missouri Synod in Canada in the projected Lutheran Council in Canada, the planning commission for the new inter-Lutheran agency for Canada included Schole and Erdman. As had been the case in the United States, the scope and functions of the agency were focused on two areas: common theological study and Christian service, a Division of Theological Studies having been incorporated into the constitution to ensure that the Council would not only engage in cooperative activities but also provide a solid theological basis on which cooperation would take place.[16] To provide staff support for this new Division, Lutheran Church–Canada arranged for Louis N. Scholl, an Ontario-born Missouri Synod pastor from Edmonton, to be called.

---

16   Threinen, *Fifty Years of Lutheran Convergence*, 133.

CHAPTER 5
Fellowship Talks

The 1958 constitution of Lutheran Church–Canada listed as one of its purposes, "To work toward doctrinal unity with other church bodies." To the extent that the Division of Theology of the Lutheran Council focused on issues on which consensus was lacking, participation in the Council might address this constitutional purpose. However, the churches did not envision working to create unity and union between the churches as a purpose for the Council; church union was viewed as a field where the church bodies felt they needed to involve themselves directly.

Regional conferences aimed at achieving union between the Lutheran bodies had been going on for many years prior to any Council. With more than half of the Lutherans in Canada without a church connection and a third of all Canadians indifferent to the call of the church, Lutheran church leaders had concluded that Canada was a vast mission field which needed to be reached. And, since all the Lutheran bodies had by now adopted English as the language of worship, competition and duplication of effort was simply not acceptable. "It is imperative that we consolidate our forces and face the future together," one of the speakers at a conference of Lutheran leaders had challenged in 1954.

These regional conferences were free conferences, attended by pastors as individuals. As a result, Missouri Synod participants often attend them without committing their church to any course of action. At one such conference in 1957, Leonard Koehler, the president of the Manitoba and Saskatchewan District, had presented a paper on

"My Conception of an Indigenous Lutheran Church in Canada." But, when Schwermann attended one such conference in 1959, he took pains to clarify that the primary goal of Missouri Synod participants was not to discuss church union. He told the conference, "We are not ready to discuss merger but we are ready to discuss doctrine and attempt to reach doctrinal agreement."[17]

To include the Missouri Synod and to encourage them officially to enter merger talks, the focus of the conferences shifted from uniting all Lutherans in Canada to seeking agreement in doctrine and practice. When agreement which led to pulpit and altar fellowship between the churches had been reached, then merger would naturally follow.

In view of the new focus, all the participants had to formally represent their church bodies. Since Lutheran Church–Canada was a federation of Districts, its participants were appointed by and ultimately responsible to their own District. The minutes of the first meeting at which official representatives began to seek agreement in doctrine and practice made this very clear. In addition to President Schole, the Lutheran Church–Canada representation was made up of H. Erdman and E. Kanning[18] from the Ontario District; L. Koehler and W. Ritter from the Manitoba and Saskatchewan District; R. Frantz and E. Fox from the Alberta-British Columbia District; and K. Riehl from the English District. But, in the joint meeting with the commissions of the other two Lutheran bodies in Canada, Lutheran Church–Canada participants functioned as a unit representing the Missouri Synod in Canada.

As the Joint Committee began its work, more deliberate steps

---

17   Threinen, *They Called Him Red*, 68.
18   Replaced by A. Stanfel the following year.

were taken to chart the course for achieving the necessary agreement: a definition of the term "Pulpit and Altar Fellowship," as understood in each of the churches; the present day basis for agreement in doctrine and practice sufficient for such fellowship among Lutherans in Canada; the procedure to be followed by each church upon agreement by representatives present at the committee; and the possible procedures or methodology to be followed in the quest for Pulpit and Altar Fellowship.

A Steering Committee of six members was established, with each Canadian church entity represented by two members, including their president. This Committee was charged with searching out and noting differences or areas of concern in doctrine and practice which may cause difficulty as the commission tried to find the road to agreement. The Committee was responsible for having theses and papers produced through inter-Lutheran subcommittees covering subjects of mutual concern which would then be studied by the entire Commission.

Areas of concern in doctrine and practice were identified by way of a questionnaire to the membership of the three churches the following year. They were: The Scriptures; Unionism; The Lodge; and Christian Ethics and Piety. Inter-Lutheran subcommittees were appointed to discuss these concerns and to come to the Joint Commission with suggestions for dealing with them.

After the 1965 meeting of the Commission, the three church presidents sent a communiqué to Lutheran clergy in Canada regarding the results of the four subcommittees. Regarding the discussion on the Scriptures, it stated, "There is remarkable agreement among us in our respective positions with regard to the doctrine of the Scriptures." Instead of a position paper on the Scriptures an enlarged sub-committee commended to the 1966 joint meeting "A Statement on The Form and Function of the Holy Scriptures" prepared earlier by the faculty of the Missouri Synod's St. Louis seminary. Regarding unionism, the communiqué stated, "We agree that great care must be exercised in all ecumenical relationships, so that our doctrinal position as Lutherans is not compromised." Regarding Lodge membership, the communiqué stated, "We all agree that lodge membership is not compatible with membership in the Christian Church but we must have redemptive concern for all men, including lodge members." Regarding Christian ethics and piety, the communiqué acknowledged that this was mainly a problem in only one of the churches. "Let not any rigid position alienate us from one another and thus from Him who loves and guides us into all truth." The communique concluded: "In these realms, we are convinced that the differences within our church bodies in Canada are just as great as the differences between the church bodies." It was a bold statement, especially since one of those who subscribed to it was the president of Lutheran Church–Canada.

The Joint Commission on Inter-Lutheran Relationships expected that its four subcommittees would formulate consensus statements in their area for approval by the entire commission and for subsequent distribution and evaluation by local inter-Lutheran ministerial conferences. But only the subcommittee on the Scriptures reported the following year and it indicated no position paper was possible at this time. In response, the Steering Committee of the Joint Commission resolved to re-examine the approaches used thus far and to seek a more productive methodology.

Rev. Thomas Ristine, LCC F President 1967.

CHAPTER 6
A Change of Vision

A period of time passed while the Council became operational. In the meantime, the Missouri Synod was re-examining its view of fellowship again. In the Brief Statement of 1932, fellowship was regarded as being possible only if people agreed on the formulation of individual doctrines. By 1950 a shift in position was apparent; the Synod accepted the Common Confession with the American Lutheran Church by affirming that "Agreement in the Gospel is foundational to church fellowship." In 1956, the Missouri Synod asked their two seminary faculties to restudy the question of fellowship, prayer fellowship, and unionism. Ultimately, out of this study, a document called Theology of Fellowship was developed which examined the Scripture passages used by the Brief Statement of 1932 to support separation. By reinterpreting the Scripture passages in the earlier document, it is apparent that the stance of the Missouri Synod on fellowship had substantially changed.

North of the border at the Tenth Convention of Lutheran Church–Canada in Kitchener, August 15-16, 1967, a new slate of officers was elected: Thomas Ristine, a pastor in London, Ontario, as president; Harold Merklinger, on the verge of retirement from the military chaplaincy, as vice-president; Maynard Pollex, now serving a congregation in Winnipeg, as secretary; Carl Wagner, as treasurer; and Don Duholke, a layman from Calgary, as member-at-large.

Ristine had only a year earlier accepted the call to be the pastor of Trinity, London; he had previously served as the Executive Secretary of the Manitoba and Saskatchewan District for nine years. His work as a District staff person for missions required him to cooperate with other Lutherans in planning missions in the District. He therefore brought to the presidency of Lutheran Church–Canada a more open attitude to other Lutherans, which he needed if he was also to provide leadership to the Lutheran Council and the Joint Commission on Inter-Lutheran Relationships. Like many people in Western Canada where he had previously served, he found the Missouri Synod's new official position on fellowship more palatable than the earlier hardline position against other Lutherans.

In addition to his leadership role in the Lutheran Council in Canada and the Joint Commission on Inter-Lutheran Relationships, one of the activities into which Ristine was drawn as president of Lutheran Church–Canada related to fellowship with the Evangelical Lutheran Church of Canada. The commissioners of the Missouri Synod and the American Lutheran Church in the United States had met to consider the possibility of formal pulpit and altar fellowship, studying the Lutheran Confessions in the light of the Holy Scriptures to see whether the two churches agreed on the teaching of the Gospel and the administration of the sacraments. Eventually, they adopted three essays which they felt reflected consensus sufficient for pulpit and altar fellowship.

Since the Evangelical Lutheran Church of Canada had been a District of the American Lutheran Church prior to January 1, 1967, it was generally assumed that the position of the District would coincide with it. However, since the former District was now a fully autonomous Church, it was appropriate that it be dealt with separately. Thus, on February 9, 1968, the Executive Committee of Lutheran Church–Canada, representing the Synod, met with the Standing Committee on Inter-church Relations of the Evangelical Lutheran Church of Canada to discuss the ramifications for Canada of the Synod's actions. By July 4, 1968, the three Districts had all passed a resolution authorizing the Committee on Relations with Other Churches of Lutheran Church–Canada to submit an appropriate recommendation to the Missouri Synod regarding the fellowship issue in Canada.

Anticipating the Missouri Synod would approve fellowship with the American Lutheran Church in 1969, the Executive Committee of Lutheran Church–Canada approved in principle a resolution re-questing the Synod also to declare pulpit and altar fellowship with the Evangelical Lutheran Church of Canada. In view of the inter-Lutheran talks under way in Canada, the resolution also asked the Synod to approve exploring the possibility of fellowship with the Lutheran Church in America – Canada Section. Based on this recommendation, the Missouri Synod at its 1969 convention proclaimed itself in pulpit and altar fellowship with the Evangelical Lutheran Church of Canada and approved exploring the possibility of fellowship with the Lutheran Church in America – Canada Section.

For many in Canada, fellowship with the Evangelical Lutheran Church of Canada was a foregone conclusion if the Synod approved fellowship with the American Lutheran Church. But the possibility of fellowship with the Lutheran Church in America – Canada Section posed some major difficulties. The Lutheran Church in America had taken the approach that doctrinal discussions were unnecessary for fellowship between Lutheran bodies; since having such discussions offered a hope for achieving pulpit and altar fellowship in Canada between the Lutheran Church in America – Canada Section and Lutheran Church–Canada, the leaders of the former had willingly participated in such talks in the context of the Joint Commission on Inter-Lutheran Relationships.

Since the discussions leading to pulpit and altar fellowship between the Synod and the American Lutheran Church had produced the desired results of fellowship, the commission, at its meeting in 1968, decided to adopt the same approach. Richard Jungkuntz, the Synod's Executive Secretary for its Commission on Theology and Church Relations, was present as a consultant and related how the essays used in the discussions between the two bodies were designed to "flush to the surface" the agreement that was present.

***

The proclamation of pulpit and altar fellowship between the Missouri Synod and the Evangelical Lutheran Church of Canada was looked upon favourably by most people within the two Western Canadian Districts of the Synod. The Alberta-British Columbia District unanimously asked George Rode, their recently-elected president, to make arrangements to hold mutual discussions on all levels and in all circuits to achieve the agreement in doctrine and practice necessary for declaring fellowship at the local level. Fully committed to the current Missouri Synod stance on fellowship indicated in the Theology of Fellowship, Rode wrote, "The attempts to formulate statements on each point of doctrine and to make these acceptable to all Lutherans have not met with great success in the past. Is it possible to recognize the true unity of the Church and to practice altar and pulpit fellowship where there is agreement concerning the doctrine of the Gospel and the administration of the Sacraments?"

The Mission Committee of the Manitoba and Saskatchewan District, confronted by a critical shortage of pastors particularly in areas of declining population, met with officials of the Evangelical Lutheran Church of Canada in January 1970 and agreed on proper protocol for serving one another's vacant parishes where feasible and requested; on the use of joint facilities; and on guidelines for congregations contemplating merger, realignment, and federation.

However, the leadership of the Ontario District had a very different reaction to the action of the Synod on fellowship. There were very few congregations of the Evangelical Lutheran Church of

Canada in the territory of the Ontario District and opposition to the Synod's proclamation on fellowship with the American Lutheran Church was substantial. Some pastors from Ontario joined the "continuation committee," formed after the Synod convention to oppose fellowship. Robert Preus, the President of the Fort Wayne seminary and the brother of Synod President Jakob Preus, prepared an essay opposing fellowship under the title, "Fellowship Reconsidered."[19] It was distributed throughout the Synod, including Canada.

Discussion of fellowship with the Evangelical Lutheran Church of Canada was further coloured by its apparent link to Synod's decision to explore fellowship with the Lutheran Church in America – Canada Section. Missouri Synod pastors and congregations had previously had negative experiences with the Lutheran Church in America in Ontario, especially with its Waterloo seminary faculty. The fact that such action would be recommended by the unity committee of Lutheran Church–Canada led to negative criticism of Lutheran Church–Canada. John Korcok, one of the more vocal pastors in the Ontario District, expressed the views of others in his District when he reported to an ad hoc gathering of about thirty-five pastors in Lethbridge, Alberta in April 1970: "On the basis of the situation at the Seminary in Waterloo, Ontario, such fellowship would be impossible. If Lutheran Church–Canada approves fellowship with the Lutheran Church in America," he contended, "twenty-nine men [pastors who shared his position] would opt out of Lutheran Church–Canada and remain with Missouri Synod."[20]

***

19   Robert D. Preus, *Fellowship Reconsidered*, 1971.

20   E. Lehman, *Notes on a Meeting of Certain Lutheran Pastors, Lethbridge, April 16, 1970*, [Report to George Rode, Alberta-British Columbia District President].

Confronted with the fact that the Evangelical Lutheran Church of Canada had declared itself to be in fellowship both with the Lutheran Church in America – Canada Section and the Missouri Synod when the latter two were not in fellowship with each other, the Joint Commission on Inter-Lutheran Relationships now attempted to close the fellowship triangle. On the assumption that consensus in doctrine and practice would likely be reached between these two Canadian entities before the parent bodies in the United States had come to a similar agreement, the Commission asked leaders of Lutheran Church–Canada: "Could pulpit and altar fellowship be declared by the Canadian entities?"

To try to achieve such pulpit and altar fellowship between Lutheran Church–Canada and the Lutheran Church in America – Canada Section, a special meeting of the Joint Commission was held May 5-6, 1970. Theodore Nickel, a vice-president of the Missouri Synod who had participated in the talks resulting in fellowship with the American Lutheran Church, was present. Small group discussions of issues alleged to be obstacles to fellowship resulted in a general agreement that the commissioners had sufficient agreement among themselves for fellowship.

A three-man committee, with staff assistance from Louis Scholl, collated and edited the documents produced by the commission which showed the basis for pulpit and altar fellowship. The committee's report entitled "Affirmation and Appeal" stated that consensus sufficient for fellowship exists and it appealed to the churches to declare and practice pulpit and altar fellowship, delaying no longer than necessary to follow orderly procedure.

A vote on the report was taken and all but two of the twenty-six commissioners supported the statement that there was sufficient consensus among themselves for pulpit and altar fellowship. Both negative votes were cast by the commissioners from Lutheran Church–Canada. Both were members of the Ontario District: Albin Stanfel, newly-elected President of the District, and Roy Knoll, who would later serve as Executive Secretary of the District.

How was it that the commissioners representing Lutheran Church–Canada were not united in their response? The answer may well be that the commissioners approached the issue from two different views on fellowship. Most of the commissioners casting "yes" votes had participated in the lengthy process of interaction and discovery. They were speaking of what they had experienced in the context of the many meetings they had attended. What they had experienced coincided with the Missouri Synod's Theology of Fellowship: basic agreement on the Gospel and the Administration of the Sacrament. The commissioners who cast "no" votes were both attending for the first time. They reflected what they had experienced in Ontario, and this coloured their own convictions regarding this issue. They approached fellowship using the more conservative approach of the Brief Statement and were convinced that agreement was required in the formulation of doctrine—and that, therefore, they and the constituency they represented did not have a basis for fellowship.

When they were pressed for clarification, the contention of the two nay-voting commissioners from Ontario was that agreement had not been achieved on women's ordination, interpretation of Scripture, and the lodge.[21] They were right. The theological land-

---

21   Stanfel had earlier been a member of the subcommittee on the lodge. The committee had agreed that there was something wrong with the lodge but its overall report had focused on issues other than lodges themselves. Stanfel had, by contrast, listed nine specific criticisms of the lodge in his minority report to the overall report.

scape had changed considerably, especially on the role of women in the church, since the early talks had occurred. The Lutheran Church in America had approved the ordination of women to the pastoral office earlier that year and, while the Evangelical Lutheran Church of Canada had not yet spoken on the issue, they were poised to do so. Faculty members in Waterloo also generally accepted the use of the "higher critical method" in exegetical courses. Since this was not generally the case in Saskatoon, commissioners from Western Canada tended to find problems with fewer of these issues.

Rev. Louis N. Scholl, LCC F President 1973.

CHAPTER 7
Another Look at Autonomy

A fter the referendum on an independent Lutheran Church–
Canada failed to pass in 1964, the Alberta-British
Columbia District had asked that another vote be taken. At
the tenth annual convention of Lutheran Church–Canada in Kitchener
from August 15-16, 1967, the delegates resurrected this idea and
approved a resolution to hold another referendum on an autonomous

Lutheran Church–Canada. To prepare for this second vote, the Executive Committee appointed a small fact-finding committee made up of: Martin Kelln, Harold Merklinger, Louis Scholl, and Theodore Schulze, Chairman, to re-study the present situation, as well as the status and future needs of Lutheran Church–Canada and report its findings to the 1968 convention.

Recognizing that the Committee could not complete its work within the prescribed time without staff assistance and aware that he would shortly be retired from the Armed Forces, Merklinger had offered to serve gratis as a field secretary for the committee for six to twelve months. The Executive Committee had accepted Merklinger's offer but provided him with an annual stipend of $1,000.

In its report—entitled "The Problems and Prospects for Lutheran Church–Canada"—the study Committee indicated it observed, as a positive development of recent years, that the image of a foreign church limited to one nationality had been lost, though Lutheran Church–Canada was still largely German in ethnic origin. The rest of the report stressed two advantages for seeking an autonomous church: one, autonomy would provide the opportunity to build a church better adapted to the changing situation in the middle of the twentieth century; and two, autonomy would provide the ability to facilitate relations with other Lutheran church bodies.

Specific arguments in favour of autonomy included the ability for members to represent themselves as Canadians rather than as a foreign church; the opportunity for members to rise to the challenge in terms of raising finances, recruitment, missions, and so forth; the ability for the Church to tailor its structure and operations to its specific needs; and a better position from which to negotiate with other church bodies. Arguments against autonomy included the caution that nationalism is an unhealthy sign in the Church; that it would sever access to present sources of manpower, leadership, and money; that it would be difficult geographically to unite the Canadian church; and that the emerging international world suggested national borders mean less and less.

By the summer of 1968, the two Districts in Western Canada had approved holding another referendum on an independent church. The Ontario District had also approved, provided the findings of the special Study Committee would be in the hands of the people three months before the vote was taken. In the meantime, Lutheran Church–Canada had asked the Synod in 1969 to grant it, together with the officials of the Synod, authority to implement autonomy for Lutheran Church–Canada, contingent on the favourable result of a forthcoming referendum of Canadian congregations. The Synod did not oppose a referendum if it was viewed as an opinion poll. It directed that the actual decision on autonomy could not be achieved through a referendum; it would require a delegate vote at the three District conventions.

The Executive Committee directed Merklinger to prepare the "pros" and "cons" of autonomy for Lutheran Church–Canada for distribution to the Canadian church by May 31, 1969. The date of March 4, 1970 was set as the deadline for when the results of the congregational poll were to be in the hands of the secretary of Lutheran Church–Canada.

To provide as much information as possible, the Board named a Special Committee for Structure and Finance to deal with questions such as: Would financial assistance continue by way of subsidy and church extension? Would the Synod supply any outright grants? Would the Synod maintain Concordia College, Edmonton? Would there be help in the form of candidates, program personnel, and materials? Further details about financial matters pertaining to autonomy would need to be obtained by the Board from various departments of Synod and added to the existing study materials prior to the vote.

The opinion poll was taken between January 1 and March 4, 1970. A total of 368 congregations were contacted, with just over half (186) responding to the poll. Of 250 pastors contacted, just over half (130) responded.

	CONGREGATIONS	CLERGY
Alberta - British Columbia District	*71.4% in favour* *(50 for, 19 against, 1 non-committed)* ***Response rate: 53%*** ***(70 replies of 132 possible)***	*72.2% in favour* *(39 for, 15 against)* ***Response rate: 55.7%*** ***(54 replies of 97 possible)***
Manitoba & Saskatchewan District	*90.6% in favour* *(48 for, 4 against, 1 tie)* ***Response rate: 53%*** ***(53 of 100 possible)***	*92.8% in favour* *(26 for, 2 against)* ***Response rate: 49.1%*** ***(28 of 57 possible)***
Ontario District	*66.7% in favour* *(36 for, 24 against)* ***Response rate: 51.7%*** ***(60 replies of 116 possible)***	*69.5% in favour* *(32 for, 14 against)* ***Response rate: 57.5%*** ***(46 replies of 80 possible)***
English & SELC Districts	*66.7% in favour* *(2 for, 1 non-committed)* ***Response rate: 15%*** ***(3 replies of 20 possible)***	*50% in favour* *(1 for, 1 against)* ***Response rate: 12.5%*** ***(2 replies of 16 possible)***
Total	*73.1% in favour* *(136 for, 47 against, 2 non-committed, 1 tie)*	*73.4% in favour* *(98 for, 32 against)*

In order to provide validity to the poll, the resolution to the Districts asked for a vote either of "for" or "against" an independent church later in 1970. Approval of the resolution at the District Conventions was to be by a simple majority. If the resolution at all the District conventions passed, Lutheran Church–Canada would hold its founding convention in September 1972 and become an autonomous church on January 16, 1973.

By 1970, however, the theological conflict within the Synod between the moderate and the conservative forces was raging. Although no pastors and few lay-people could remain neutral in the conflict, it was particularly evident in the Ontario District. The declaration of fellowship with the Evangelical Lutheran Church of Canada, coupled with permission the previous year for women to vote in church assemblies, had resulted in two pastors and a large congregation in Ottawa leaving the Missouri Synod and joining the more conservative Wisconsin Synod. Al Stanfel had been named associate executive secretary of the District early in 1969 to assist Horace Erdman who was scheduled to retire three years hence. Stanfel was on the slate for president, along with Tom Ristine, who had been a District vice-president and was concluding his term as president of Lutheran Church–Canada. According to the June 15, 1970, edition of the London Free Press, Stanfel had identified himself as a conservative and Ristine had identified himself as a moderate.

In the end, Stanfel was elected as president and the vote on autonomy for Lutheran Church–Canada was again thwarted: seventy of the delegates had voted in favour of autonomy and sixty-four delegates had voted against. But, prior to the vote, the delegates had decided it would take a two-thirds majority for the vote to pass in the

District. Following the vote, Ristine declared: "Autonomy is now a dead issue."

***

While this drama was unfolding in Ontario, Western Canada was focused on pastoral training. The issue of pastoral training was not new. At a meeting between representative of Lutheran Church–Canada and the Missouri Synod in October 1964, these questions had arisen: "Can a church body be self-governing if it is not truly self-propagating and self-supporting? Can the Canadian Church be independent if it does not have provision for pastoral preparation?"

Since its very first meeting in 1958, pastoral preparation for the Canadian Church had been on the agenda of Lutheran Church–Canada. A committee of Walter Wangerin, president of Concordia College; Albert Oppertshauser, a layman in the Edmonton area; and George Rode, pastor of Grace, Edmonton, had been appointed to study the advantages of a Lutheran seminary in Canada. The committee had reported that the establishment of a seminary was necessary for these reasons: the distances involved for Canadian students to attend seminary in the United States; the successful experiences of other Lutheran bodies now operating seminaries in Canada; and the synodical policy to establish seminaries outside the U.S.A. for the training of a native ministry. For an indigenous church, a seminary is an essential part, the committee had stated, since many pastors with American citizenship return to their native land after a short ministry in Canada. David Appelt, one of the Board members had also gathered information from church bodies in Canada as to the standards for the education of theological students.

On January 23, 1965, the Committee on Higher Education again wrestled with this issue. Up to this time, Canadian students had been getting their pastoral training at the two Missouri Synod seminaries in the United States. Anyone who attended a Lutheran seminary of another Lutheran body in Canada would, after graduation, not receive a call to serve in the Missouri Synod. But the growth of Canadian nationalism in the 1960s had prompted many potential ministerial students from the Missouri Synod in Canada to ask why the Synod did not have a seminary program in Canada. In addition, the restrictions for a Canadian to work while studying in the United States had made attendance at a Missouri Synod seminary prohibitively expensive.

As the Committee examined the objections of Missouri Synod seminarians to studying in the United States, several reasons were identified. Among them: a reluctance to study in a foreign country. Committee member Harold Merklinger noted other problems with Canadians studying in American seminaries: there is a "Canadian idiom"; many Canadians are vulnerable to calls to American churches where development is further advanced than in Canada; Canadian men may marry American women which results in a "pull" back to the United States; classmates suggest eligible Canadian candidates for openings in American churches which results in a "brain-drain" for the Canadian church; and there is a "brain-washing" of Canadian students in American seminaries which presents problems for serving in Canada.

Coincidentally, in March 1966, the Board of Governors of Lutheran Theological Seminary in Saskatoon had invited Lutheran Church–Canada to explore the possibilities of some form of cooperative endeavour in theological education in the projected development of Lutheran Theological Seminary in Saskatoon.

With these developments as background, delegates to the tenth annual convention of Lutheran Church–Canada in 1967 passed a resolution requesting a thorough study of every phase of activity in view of autonomy, including pastoral preparation. To accomplish the latter, the Board of Directors asked the Synod's Board for Higher Education to provide a capable person to examine the feasibility of establishing a training program for full-time church workers in Canada.

The study which resulted began with two assumptions: an indigenous church must train its own clergy if it is to flourish or even survive; and the clergy must be acquainted with, and to some extent identify with, the history and culture of the people they serve and those whom they hope to win. On the basis of these assumptions, the study committee had examined five ways by which an autonomous church could educate its theological students: one, continue to use the St. Louis and Springfield seminaries (Missouri Synod); two, provide a duplication in Canada of the programs of these schools; three, establish one or more "Houses of Study"; four, arrange for students to pursue "itinerant" study at various schools; five, use the two existing Lutheran seminaries in Canada (Saskatoon and Waterloo). The study favoured the fifth approach since these schools followed the curriculum and used the same or similar entrance requirements to those then in use in Missouri Synod seminaries.

It is significant to note that, in response to the findings of the Committee, Synod president Oliver Harms urged Lutheran Church–Canada to give serious consideration to the invitation of the Saskatoon and Waterloo seminaries to provide theological education to its students. On March 23, 1968, Schole and Merklinger met with the Study Committee to map out a working plan. As an initial step toward the achievement of the goal, the Committee felt that an arrangement should be worked out in which students, particularly from Western Canada, would be trained at the Lutheran Theological Seminary in Saskatoon. The training of these students would be under the supervision of the Synod's Board for Higher Education, operating through either the St. Louis or the Springfield seminary, with Synod faculty members teaching some courses. The Committee also decided to explore the possibility of a similar arrangement to meet the needs of Lutheran Church–Canada students in Eastern Canada.

Logistically, the Committee discussed the possibility that students might enrol in the Saskatoon seminary on a fee basis at the seminary and be ordained after successfully passing a colloquy. Alternatively, Lutheran Church–Canada could make a per capita contribution to the seminary for each student or rent facilities at the seminary but provide its own teaching staff with the possibility of some overlapping of courses. The program would be under its own administration or be a branch seminary of Springfield or St. Louis. As a third alternative to the above, Lutheran Church–Canada might become a full partner with the other Lutheran bodies in Western Canada and support the seminary on a per communicant basis.

While the Committee had been attempting to work out an acceptable plan of action for training Lutheran Church–Canada pastors in Canada, Missouri Synod students began independently to enrol at the Saskatoon seminary. This increased the pressure to solve the problem of providing theological education in Western Canada, and the Manitoba and Saskatchewan District urged Lutheran Church–Canada to proceed with all possible haste to provide theological education for prospective Canadian ministerial students. Since the Saskatoon option presented by the study committee appeared to offer the best possibility, the twelfth convention of Lutheran Church–Canada on September 23-25, 1969, urged its implementation. On November 10, the Board recommended that a committee be formed to formulate ways and means of implementing the convention resolution.

At the beginning of January 1970, the newly-elected President of the Missouri Synod, Jacob Preus, also appeared to favour having Lutheran Church–Canada students attend the Saskatoon seminary. He appointed a committee to study the feasibility of doing so and to examine the requirements governing their admission to the ministry of the Synod. But by March 9, 1970, the Synod's Board of Higher Education, which had responsibility for supervising the theological education of students preparing for ministry in the Missouri Synod, had not officially indicated to Lutheran Church–Canada a course of action which it should follow. Concerned that the students were putting their admission into the Missouri Synod ministry in jeopardy by attending the Saskatoon seminary, the Board of Directors of Lutheran Church–Canada asked the three Canadian Districts to consider as an interim measure providing financial aid to Missouri Synod students at the Saskatoon institution willing to transfer to one of the Synod's seminaries for their final year of study. By doing so, they assumed they would be eligible on graduation for a call into the Synod.

In September 1970, the delegates to the thirteenth convention of Lutheran Church–Canada were informed that, since Missouri Synod students from Canada were attending Lutheran Theological

Seminary in Saskatoon, the Manitoba and Saskatchewan District had decided to ask Lutheran Church–Canada and the Board of Directors of the Missouri Synod to establish a Canadian seminary as a future consideration and to consider the establishment immediately of a chair of theology at the Saskatoon seminary. To help implement the latter, the District was ready to underwrite the cost of such a chair in conjunction with the Synod.

CHAPTER 8
Changed Times

New officers elected for Lutheran Church–Canada at its 1970 convention were: Harold Merklinger, president and Carl Wagner, treasurer. The three Canadian District Presidents filled the offices of vice-president, secretary, and member-at-large. The new Board of Directors was confronted with a number of serious issues, complicated by the fact that Oliver Harms had been replaced by Jacob Preus as president of the Missouri Synod, and the fact that conflict within the Synod between moderates and conservatives was continuing to build up.

While the concept of an autonomous Lutheran Church–Canada had initially been Merklinger's idea and while he had also been actively involved in much of its subsequent development, it was tragically during his presidency that it reached its lowest point. Following the disheartening failure of the vote on autonomy in the Ontario District for a second time, the Board of Directors on March 1, 1971, recommended that changes in the Articles and Bylaws of Lutheran Church–Canada be made to scale back the structure to those aspects which were absolutely essential for it to retain its Dominion charter.

In addition, in the interest of saving time and money, the Board decided to hold the next convention during a free evening at the upcoming convention of the Synod in Milwaukee, the delegates to be selected from among the Canadian delegates to the Synod convention. The main item on the agenda of the convention of Lutheran Church–Canada was the adoption of a revised draft constitution. One of the revisions called for conventions to be reduced in frequency from annually to every two years, and for the terms of officers to be increased in length from three to four years.

***

Although the continued existence of Lutheran Church–Canada as an entity was in doubt, its Board of Directors attempted to move ahead on the question of seminary education in Canada. On November 11-12, 1970, a meeting to discuss the issue took place in Saskatoon between Missouri Synod Vice-President Roland Wieder-aenders, the three Canadian District Presidents, and the President of Lutheran Church–Canada. At the meeting, Wiederaenders pointed out that the Missouri Synod students at Lutheran Theological Seminary in Saskatoon did not fit the Synod's pastor-training program. In view of this fact, he said new options would need to be opened. He had supported the suggestion of the Manitoba and Saskatchewan District board to establish a Chair of Theology at the seminary in Saskatoon. This essentially meant that the Missouri Synod would place a professor at that institution.

"He should not be a young man," thought Wiederaenders. "He should be a man who would influence the school's theological attitude, give special guidance to Missouri Synod students and serve as a friend, as well. At the time of vicarage, he would certify the potential vicar after he has been examined informally by the three District Presidents to determine his attitude, doctrinal position, aims, likes, etc. Then the student would be recommended to the Council of Presidents for vicarage assignment."

Wiederaenders continued: "The student would be under the Synod's professor at Saskatoon during his vicarage year and after his vicarage would return to the seminary in Saskatoon. He would graduate with the seminary's diploma and, with the Synod professor's recommendation, meet again with the three District Presidents to determine qualifications for a call into the ministry of the Missouri Synod. The Synod's professor and the three District Presidents would then recommend the student to the Council of Presidents for placement together with other students from the Missouri Synod's seminaries. The vicarage and candidate placement would not necessarily be in Canada."

Acting on an overture submitted by the Manitoba and Saskatchewan District board, the Synod at its convention in Milwaukee in July 1971 established the Chair of Theology in Saskatoon. It neglected, however, to provide for the orderly acceptance of the graduates of that program into the Synod. In view of the controversy raging in the Synod, the Board for Higher Education was apparently unable or unwilling to help and assist in solving this aspect of the problem in the Saskatoon proposal. Regardless, since the Synod had taken action to establish the Chair of Theology, the Board of Directors of Lutheran Church–Canada decided to implement it by asking Roland Frantz, the president of Concordia College, to serve temporarily as the Missouri Synod professor to fill the Chair of Theology on a part-time basis. By travelling to Saskatoon one day a week, teaching a course, and meeting with the Missouri Synod students at the seminary, he launched the Chair of Theology.

In 1973, Walter Koehler, an Alberta pastor with a Th. D. from the Synod's St. Louis seminary, was called to serve in this capacity on a permanent basis. To provide for the orderly acceptance of graduates, candidates were interviewed by the Synod's Colloquy Committee and the Canadian District Presidents, after which they were placed for service in the church by the Synod's Council of Presidents.

Meanwhile, the Synod's action to establish a Chair of Theology in Saskatoon was strongly opposed, especially by a number of pastors in Ontario. Those who opposed it pointed out that Koehler's doctorate was in counselling and the courses he was teaching were in the practical rather than the systematic area, where the differences between the Lutheran bodies were more likely to surface. When supporters of the Saskatoon arrangement identified a second Missouri Synod faculty person to counter the criticism of the gainsayers, the Synod's Board for Higher Education delayed issuing that call.

***

Another issue which confronted the new Board of Directors elected in 1970 was the question of investigating "the possibility of fellowship with the Lutheran Church in America – Canada Section." A year earlier, when the Synod declared fellowship with the Evangelical Lutheran Church of Canada, it had also approved investigating the possibility of broader fellowship. While the non-Missouri Synod members of the Joint Commission on Inter-Lutheran Relationship were encouraged by this action of the Synod, they now asked how the Missouri Synod could declare pulpit and altar fellowship with only a part of the Lutheran Church in America without being in fellowship with the entire body.

Merklinger, in turn, passed the question on to the Synod's Commission on Constitutional Matters for an official answer. When the Commission failed to respond, Merklinger persisted. "We are convinced that the Denver and Milwaukee conventions [of the Synod] would not encourage us to pursue an exercise in futility. However, at the moment, we cannot see our way through this issue without the

Commission's help."[22]

Finally, the Executive Secretary of the Commission responded, "A declaration of pulpit and altar fellowship by three Districts of The Lutheran Church–Canada with the LCA-Canada Section would be contrary to the [Synod's] bylaws." Then he added, "Synod has indicated its interest in declaring pulpit and altar fellowship in Canada when the time is right."[23] When Ralph Bohlmann, Executive Secretary of the Synod's Commission on Theology and Church Relations at the time, received a copy of the Merklinger correspondence, he was more sympathetic. He pointed out that the Canadian situation posed a dilemma and encouraged the Commission on Constitutional Matters to be more helpful. Finally, the Commission ruled, "Under its present bylaws the Synod cannot establish fellowship with a 'section' of another church body," adding after this formal ruling: "Bylaws, of course, can be amended quite readily by the Synod."[24]

***

After three frustrating and largely unproductive years for the development of Lutheran Church–Canada, Merklinger retired and turned things over to a new leader in February 1973. Louis Scholl, who had left his position with the Lutheran Council in Canada in 1971 to accept a call to a congregation in Windsor, was elected president; Philip Fry, the newly-elected President of the Manitoba and Saskatchewan District was elected vice-president; George Rode, President of the Alberta-British Columbia Districts was elected secretary; Robert Pippus became treasurer; and Henry Baker of Regina and Albin Stanfel, President of the Ontario District, became members-at-large.

---

22   Merklinger to Herbert Mueller, November 25, 1971.
23   Mueller to Merklinger, February 15, 1972.
24   Mueller to Bohlmann, May 15, 1972.

Lutheran Church–Canada could not have found a more qualified person to serve as its president. Scholl's five years with the Council had provided him with a unique insider's understanding of Lutheran Church–Canada and the whole inter-Lutheran scene. In his letter announcing the first meeting of the Board of Directors on March 8, 1973, he signalled a change for the better when he wrote, "I hope we will also have time to assess the climate in which Lutheran Church–Canada presently finds itself and ways in which this agency can serve as a more effective forum for cooperation in the task our Districts have in common."

In Scholl's first report to a convention of Lutheran Church–Canada in 1975, he evaluated several areas of concern and suggested solutions for them. Among them was the concept of Lutheran Church–Canada as an administrative unit. "It is difficult to describe how, if at all, Synod's relation to the Canadian scene changed as a result of declaring Lutheran Church–Canada its administrative arm in Canada," Scholl wrote. He called for consultation with appropriate synodical staff to identify more clearly the ways in which Lutheran Church–Canada could be of greater service as the administrative arm of the Missouri Synod in Canada. He also felt that Lutheran Church–Canada should have access to conventions of the Synod through the right to submit overtures.

Another concern which Scholl raised related to the still unresolved question of how fellowship with the Lutheran Church in America – Canada Section could be achieved. "The simplest solution would be for Synod to grant Lutheran Church–Canada the authority not only to negotiate fellowship and merger, but also to consummate that fellowship and merger if and when, by the Spirit's grace, we arrive at and affirm the consensus that under-girds true unity," he wrote.

As a final concern, Scholl pointed out that the Missouri Synod had consistently over the years failed to provide Lutheran Church–Canada with the funds needed to cover its share of the work which it was doing together with the other two Lutheran bodies in the Lutheran Council in Canada. While the other two bodies were paying their share in full, the Synod was often short and late in its apportionment. "All this is not fair to our partners," Scholl pointed out.

On March 17-18, 1976, a special meeting of the Board of Directors was held with three members of the Synod's Board of Directors. The direction indicated by the meeting was that Lutheran Church–Canada should be played down as an administrative unit; and that Lutheran Church–Canada should take over funding for the Lutheran Council in Canada on an increasing scale.

On the matter of establishing fellowship with the Lutheran Church in America – Canada Section, the participants in the special meeting were of the opinion that, since it was unlikely the Synod would allow the Districts in Canada to establish fellowship with the Lutheran Church in America – Canada Section on their own, Missouri Synod congregations in Canada should form an indigenous church which would be free to negotiate merger or strive to establish fellowship with the Lutheran Church in America – Canada Section.

A year later, the matter came to the convention of the Synod which resolved "that the Commission on Constitutional Matters, the CTCR, and the Canadian District Presidents study the advisability of amending the Synod's Bylaws to grant Canadian Districts the authority to negotiate toward fellowship in Canada through Lutheran

Church–Canada and report to the next convention." Since it was anticipated that Lutheran Church–Canada would request the privilege of forming an indigenous sister church in Canada in 1979, no further action was felt necessary on this resolution; the question of fellowship would then become the responsibility of the new sister church body.

***

While activities relating to Lutheran Church–Canada autonomy, the Lutheran Council in Canada, and discussions of altar and pulpit fellowship were under way, events had occurred in the Missouri Synod which had a direct bearing on Lutheran Church–Canada. Although some people in Canada had hoped that the Canadian church might be able to chart an independent course from what was happening south of the border, this proved not to be possible. The Districts in Canada were still part of the Synod in every sense of the word: delegates to the Missouri Synod conventions still included Canadians; many pastors in Canada had received their theological training at Missouri Synod seminaries; and the network of relationships between Canadians and the rest of the Missouri Synod was extensive.

A struggle between moderates and conservatives for dominance in the Missouri Synod had been mounting for several years. Subsequent to the 1962 convention of the Synod, it became common knowledge that a vigorous conservative element in the church was organizing itself as a political force to direct future decisions of the Synod. This had led in 1969 to the unseating of Oliver Harms as President of the Synod in favour of Jacob Preus. The struggle intensified and in 1973 broke out in open conflict at the Missouri Synod convention in New Orleans. Commenting on the convention,

Alberta-British Columbia District President George Rode wrote: "There was an apparent impatience with anyone who expressed a view different from that which we have always held; a lack of brotherly conduct in dealing with the issues at the seminary; a failure to listen, to understand, to learn."

Following the New Orleans convention, matters went from bad to worse. In February 1974, John Tietjen, the president of the St. Louis seminary, was suspended and the vast majority of the students walked out to show their support for him. In support of the students, forty-five members of a fifty-member faculty joined them and were dismissed. Together, the former students and the dismissed faculty formed a seminary-in-exile (Seminex). Because the new institution had not been approved by the Synod, the decision to form Seminex brought into question whether and how its vicars and graduates could serve within the Missouri Synod. It was a question which sent ripples throughout the Synod, including the Canadian Districts.

Rode and Fry were among the District presidents who took a sympathetic approach to their placement. Commenting on the attempts to clear the way for these students to enter the ministerium of the Missouri Synod, Rode told his District in 1974, "I am very eager to have these gifts of God placed into a church body, sorely in need of full-time workers.... I am also concerned that all things be done in an orderly way."

Other District Presidents in the Missouri Synod disagreed with Rode. Among them was Albin Stanfel in Ontario, who took a hard line against vicars and graduates of Seminex coming to serve congregations in the District. As a result, a few pastors and their congregations left the Ontario District. Some of them joined the English

District which took a more moderate approach to Seminex. Others left the Missouri Synod entirely to become independent, later to join one of the other two Lutheran bodies in Canada. Among the latter were Tom Ristine and his congregation in London, Ontario.

***

The student walk-out from the St. Louis seminary and the formation of Seminex deprived the Missouri Synod of a large number of potential pastoral graduates. For years the Canadian Districts had relied annually on an influx of seminary graduates to fill their pastoral needs. Leonard Koehler, the president of the Manitoba and Saskatchewan District, had reported in 1961 that one third of the congregations in his District were vacant. The same year, Philip Fiess, the President of the Ontario District, had pointed out that the three Canadian Districts had asked for twenty-four graduates that year. Ten years later, not a great deal had changed. George Rode talked about "a church body, sorely in need of full-time workers."

The Chair of Theology, which the Synod had established at Lutheran Theological Seminary in Saskatoon in 1971, addressed both the desire of Canadians for a pastoral training opportunity in Canada and the perpetual shortage of pastors. But many who identified with the more conservative views within the Synod had grave concerns about this approach to preparing pastors for the Canadian Church. They maintained that the Saskatoon arrangement would not provide sufficient control over the doctrine taught to future graduates. In their view, it constituted a dangerous precedent.

In an attempt to reverse the Synod's decision to establish a Chair of Theology at the Saskatoon seminary, several pastors in the Ontario District asked the Synod's Commission on Constitutional Matters to rule on the constitutionality of the 1971 decision. But the Commission had become immobilized by the synodical controversy and failed to act. Anxious to move the matter along, the Ontario District asked the Synod's Board of Higher Education to give serious consideration to establishing a branch seminary in Ontario attached to one of the Missouri Synod seminaries in the United States.

In January 1974, the Board of Directors of the District took matters into their own hands and named a task force to investigate the possibilities of establishing such a branch seminary. It consisting of Roger Humann, who had earlier served as a campus chaplain in Saskatoon and was now the pastor of Resurrection Lutheran Church in St. Catharines; Mervin Huras, a pastor in Elmira; and John Daniels, a prominent Ontario layman. The task force pointed to the need for some sort of seminary program for Ontario. It recommended that it be an extension centre of the Springfield seminary[25] and be located near an Ontario University. In 1975, the Synod approved the plan and the following year it was established in the facilities of Resurrection Lutheran Church. Roger Humann was named Dean of the institution and a member of the Fort Wayne seminary faculty, together with area pastors from southern Ontario constituting the initial teaching staff.

***

When the Board of Directors of Lutheran Church–Canada met in November 1976, it was apparent that the Ontario District was beginning to disassociate itself from the direction Lutheran Church–Canada was taking. Albin Stanfel, the President of the District, was absent even though the meeting was being held in Toronto.

---

25   Subsequently moved to the former campus of the Synod's senior college in Fort Wayne.

The treasurer reported that Lutheran Church–Canada owed about $6,000 on its share for the Joint Commission on Inter-Lutheran Relationships, partly because no funds had been received from the Ontario District. The Ontario District representatives to the Commission declared inadequate a statement on the Scriptures which had been prepared by a subcommittee of the Lutheran Church–Canada Commissioners; the Ontario District Convention adopted eight theses with antithesis to take its place.

Scholl talked about "the uncertainty of the future of Lutheran Church–Canada" and referred to the next convention as "important for the future direction of Lutheran Church–Canada." When Lutheran Church–Canada met in convention in Mississauga, Ontario from March 7-9, 1977, Scholl declined to be nominated as president.

***

In 1977, as the merger process through the Joint Commission on Inter-Lutheran Relationships reached the mid-point of the timetable it had projected in 1973, there was little hope among Lutheran Church–Canada participants in the talks that merger with other Lutherans in Canada could occur. This was due to the actions taken by the various bodies on the issue of whether women could be ordained to the pastoral ministry. The other Lutheran bodies in Canada had committed themselves to permitting it and the Missouri Synod had repeated its position that faithfulness to the Scriptures would not allow it. When a compromise was proposed that in the merged church the practice of ordaining both men and women be allowed and that congregations be given the right to select their own pastor, male or female, Commission members from Lutheran Church–Canada either voted in opposition or abstained from voting. The vote acknowledged that the three-way Lutheran merger process had come to an end. The two bodies which had approved the ordination of women to the pastoral office proceeded to undertake a two-way merger, without the active participation of Lutheran Church–Canada. While some interested members of Lutheran Church–Canada continued to attend meetings of the Joint Commission as visitors for a while, it no longer sent official commissioners.

***

The breakdown in merger talks in Canada meant that the theological basis upon which fellowship between the Missouri Synod and the Evangelical Lutheran Church of Canada had been built was in question. It was, therefore, important to clarify the comparative theological stances of the two churches at the church body level. To provide such clarification, a special committee of representatives of the two Churches was formed in 1977. Recognizing that the 1969 fellowship action of the Churches only affected the Canadian Churches, three of the four Missouri Synod committee members were from Lutheran Church–Canada: Elroy Treit, Ed Lehman, and Allan Schade.[26]

For various reasons, the committee did not meet until 1982. After meeting on four separate occasions, the committee issued a general summary of the areas of agreement and divergence between the two churches.[27] While it acknowledged many areas of agreement, it also recognized that there were significant unresolved differences. The fact that the Evangelical Lutheran Church of Canada would admit women to the office of the pastoral ministry on the basis of its understanding

26   The fourth member was Sam Nafzger, Executive Secretary of the Synod's Commission on Theology and Church Relations.
27   "A Summary Statement of Agreement and Differences," *The Canadian Lutheran*, September 1984: 1-2.

of the Scriptures and that the Missouri Synod would not do so on the basis of its understanding of the Scriptures was a strong indication that the respective Churches took different approaches to the interpretation of Scripture. This, even more than the differing views on the ordination of women, caused the committee to conclude that the basis for pulpit and altar fellowship proclaimed by the two Churches in 1969 was lacking. As Treit stated in his "Introduction" to the 1984 *A Summary Statement*: "We do not have agreement on some very basic doctrines of the church. The primary difference is in the matter of the Scriptures themselves."

Since the Evangelical Lutheran Church of Canada disappeared through a merger with the Lutheran Church in America – Canada Section the following year, pulpit and altar fellowship between the Missouri Synod and the Evangelical Lutheran Church of Canada would cease to exist after 1985, in any case.

CHAPTER 9
Back on Track

R eturning to the story of the internal development of Lutheran Church–Canada, when delegates met in convention in 1977, they faced problems in identity, purpose, and direction. They were confronted by four options: retain the status quo; phase down; expand and strengthen Lutheran Church–Canada; or attain autonomy and independence. After discussing the options in groups and in the plenary, the consensus was that the first two options were not viable. Lutheran Church–Canada had to move to the third option with the fourth option as its goal.

While the future was unclear for Lutheran Church–Canada in many respects, the fact that merger with the other Lutheran bodies was no longer an option for the Missouri Synod in Canada had a positive effect on the participants at the convention. It allowed the delegates to relax and focus their attention on what specifically to do about Lutheran Church–Canada. It also reduced the sharp East-West divisions which had existed throughout much of its history. Without the option of merger, the participants regained new hope that an autonomous Lutheran Church–Canada was possible. As the Missouri Synod representative at the convention reported to President Jacob Preus, the spirit of the gathering "seemed good; better than on previous occasions." There were even "better relationships between the east and west."

The difference in mood was also reflected in the election of Elroy Treit, a Vancouver-based pastor, as president. Although he was a newcomer to the proceedings of Lutheran Church–Canada, he set an optimistic tone for better times under his presidency. In a letter to President Preus, following the convention, Treit wrote, "The presidency of the Lutheran Church–Canada is now in new hands and the directions are going to be altered accordingly."

Treit blamed the reason for Lutheran Church–Canada's current state on leadership which had gotten caught up in inter-synodical friendships, blinding them to things that were happening to the Missouri Synod in Canada. "With the new interest and the new thrust of the LCC, I know that the feelings are now pointed to the independent, indigenous, conservative Lutheran church body here," he wrote.[28]

While it is true that much of the energy of the leadership had become channelled into forming a Canadian Lutheran Church in union with other Lutherans, it should be noted that the direction had been taken all along the way with the knowledge and approval of the Missouri Synod and its leadership. Harold Merklinger had a saying that Canadians of the Missouri Synod had a tendency of looking over their shoulders to make sure their actions were not at variance with what the Synod leadership approved. This cautionary attitude was a strong characteristic in the life of the federation which was Lutheran Church–Canada.

Although the impetus for the formation of Lutheran Church–Canada had grown out of a recognition that the Missouri Synod constituency in Canada had a unique identity, its connection with the Missouri Synod had largely determined its actions. For Lutheran Church–Canada to come into being, the three Canadian District presidents of the Missouri Synod had to authorize it. And after it was

---

28   Elroy Treit to J. A. O. Preus, April 26, 1977.

formed, Schwermann had taken great pains to assure the Synod that it did not change the relationship of its Districts and congregations in Canada to the Synod: the delegates to its conventions were named by these Districts, and their Presidents often sat on the Board of Directors. As a result, there were few actions which Lutheran Church–Canada took which the Synod had not approved. In planning for seminary education in Canada, for example, the leadership of the Synod had proposed on separate occasions that Canadian students might attend the seminary in Saskatoon. Likewise, guided by the reports which they were receiving, the same Synodical leadership encouraged Lutheran Church–Canada to look to fellowship and a possible merger with other Lutherans.

For a period of time, therefore, the energy which had initially gone into developing an independent Lutheran Church–Canada in fellowship with the Missouri Synod was channelled into cooperative Lutheran ministry and planning for a pan-Lutheran Church in Canada. Among those who supported the concept of an inclusive Lutheran Church in Canada was a former mission director, Thomas Ristine, who had seen the futility of Lutheran bodies going it alone on the Canadian prairies. Among those who also supported the concept were George Rode and Phil Fry, District presidents who had struggled to provide pastoral candidates for vacant prairie parishes. It is significant that Rode and Fry both had their roots in Western Canada where they had also served parishes. But with their departure from the scene, the stage was set for new leaders with a renewed vision for an independent Lutheran Church–Canada in fellowship with the Missouri Synod. It was a new thrust which was possible because it was the position which the Synod had assumed following the election of Jakob Preus to the presidency in 1969.

***

In many ways, Elroy Treit was an unusual choice for the presidency of Lutheran Church–Canada. Although he had been a successful pastor and served a growing congregation, he presented a very different presidential image from that to which most people were accustomed.

But it soon became evident that if Lutheran Church–Canada was to succeed, it needed a president with his passion. In his inimitable way, Treit challenged the delegates at the convention not to close down Lutheran Church–Canada, nor to stay the same, but to expand its work. He later shared that his challenge was specifically intended to wake the delegates from their lethargy and to motivate them to join him in working toward the goal of autonomy for Lutheran Church–Canada, simply because it was the right thing to do.

Treit's challenge was precisely what the convention delegates needed. It also turned out to be what the majority of the pastors and congregations of Lutheran Church–Canada needed. The breakdown in merger talks had left many of them reeling with indecision. Many were not happy that the merger had failed but Treit's challenge gave them something else positive to pursue.

At the suggestion of the new Board of Directors, the convention appointed a Task Force to determine with a degree of certainty the will of the Missouri Synod congregations in Canada. By conducting a sample survey of pastors and communicant members of Missouri Synod congregations in Canada, the Task Force was to ask first and foremost whether or not the members of the Church as a whole favoured forming an indigenous Lutheran Church–Canada, as a sister church to the Missouri Synod. This analysis should include a reference to both an indigenous church and a possible merged church. To accomplish its task in a professional manner, the Task Force engaged Arctic Mackenzie Consultants.

While the survey indicated there was residual support for being part of a merged church, there was strong support for the idea of an indigenous church from pastors and lay persons from all kinds of congregations from across the country. Based on the positive results of the survey, the Board of Directors recommended that the Canadian Districts take a vote on the formation of a self-governing indigenous Lutheran Church–Canada at their forthcoming conventions.

In the spring of 1978, each of the three Districts voted by more than 90 percent to ask Lutheran Church–Canada to move toward autonomy and authorized the Board of Directors of Lutheran Church–Canada to initiate and carry out the process by which an indigenous church could come into being. Each District also approved sending overtures to the 1979 convention of the Missouri Synod in Dallas, asking for approval to form a self-governing, indigenous Lutheran Church in Canada.

The 1978 District conventions were important for the story of Lutheran Church–Canada's development because they mark the beginning of decisive action toward an autonomous church. Edwin Lehman was elected as the successor to George Rode in the Alberta-British Columbia District and Roy Holm as the successor to Phil Fry in the Manitoba and Saskatchewan District. Both of these new District Presidents were staunch supporters of an independent Lutheran Church–Canada. Albin Stanfel, who was re-elected as President of the Ontario District, had also become a supporter of the formation of an independent Church in Canada by this time. As the self-governing, indigenous Lutheran Church–Canada came into being, it was these men who served with Treit on its Board of Directors and therefore provided the leadership and planning for the new independent Church.

At its September 7-8, 1978 meeting, the newly-constituted Board of Directors appointed a Ways and Means Committee. Reminiscent of the Study Committee eighteen years earlier, it was comprised by Members of the Board of Directors; Executives of the Canadian Districts; and Representatives of the English, Minnesota North, and SELC Districts. Its purpose was to plan for the birth of the new church. Six study committees were identified: home and foreign missions, chaired by Roy Holm; theological basis and church relations, chaired by Edwin Lehman; higher education and seminary training, chaired by Richard Ballenthin; parish services and auxiliaries, chaired by Lester Gierach; legal and financial matters, chaired by Albin Stanfel; and constitution and structure, chaired by Elroy Treit.

From January 16-17, 1979, twelve members of the Ways and Means Committee met in a retreat centre in Mississauga, Ontario. Various thoughts were shared by the committee members. Among them were the following:

• It's good to have those responsible for doing the work and directing it to be as close as possible to the people of the church. We have had recent examples of projects that have done very well once they came under the direction of Canadians.

• An indigenous Lutheran Church–Canada would be able better to face the challenge of serving in Canada.

• If we were an indigenous Lutheran Church–Canada, we would

have a better opportunity to stand for good, sound Lutheranism in Canada. We could give congregations an alternative.

• Since the other two Lutheran Churches in Canada are merging, we can better contribute our light to them as a national church rather than a foreign church.

• As an indigenous church we could better serve the kingdom of God. We have one purpose for existence on earth, to proclaim the Gospel.

• If Lutheran Church–Canada can help proclaim the Gospel, then we really need it.

• Our nation is just finding its identity. Our needs are different than those in the United States. If we fail, it must be because we tried and it wasn't the Lord's time—not because we didn't try.

Objections to forming Lutheran Church–Canada were also shared. These included increased administrative costs; loss of the benefits of the association over the years with people of the Missouri Synod; fear of change; fear of a narrowed church culture; and the question of whether there is enough theological and administrative leadership.

Carl Wagner, the Executive Director of the Manitoba and Saskatchewan District, was named chairman of the entire Committee. In terms of the timetable, the committee optimistically aimed at having preliminary reports by May 1979 and a model later in November. This model was to be presented to a convention of Lutheran Church–Canada; then to a national conference of pastors and lay leaders early in 1980 to acquaint the constituency with it; then for action by the 1980 District conventions; and finally for approval to the convention of the Synod in 1981.

Wagner felt it would take at least two years for the transition from the present status to that of a fully organized Lutheran Church–Canada.[29] A part-time, temporary staff assistant would likely be needed to research and work out the necessary details. Two successive annual conventions of Lutheran Church–Canada would approve proposed actions of the Board of Directors.

***

The Ways and Means Committee met in Winnipeg as projected May 7-9, 1979. Eighteen members of the Committee, plus President Preus and two other staff persons from the Missouri Synod, were in attendance. Preus recounted the present trend for Districts, such as in Brazil, to form partner churches of the Missouri Synod. He indicated that resolutions of the Synod pertaining to independence must be a Canadian decision. Therefore, he suggested consulting with officials of the Evangelical Lutheran Church of Canada regarding its experience in becoming an independent church in Canada.

The meeting in May was a working meeting. Subcommittees studied the issues, submitted proposals, and received reactions. Individuals demonstrated a strong commitment towards an autonomous Lutheran Church–Canada, based on frank discussion of the issues and a willingness to make choices based on the common good.

Optimistic that the goal of an autonomous church in Canada could be achieved, Lutheran Church–Canada reported to the 1979 convention of the Missouri Synod that there was strong support for the formation of a self-governing, indigenous Church. In response, the Synod encouraged Lutheran Church–Canada to move ahead according to the schedule it had proposed.

***

---

29   In actual fact, it took three times that long.

Each subcommittee faced the challenge of what the new church should look like and what it should do. Included in the deliberations of one of the subcommittees was the question of structure. For its entire lifetime, Lutheran Church–Canada had functioned with a structure comprised of three geographical Districts created by the Missouri Synod. But these Districts had united to create Lutheran Church–Canada, giving them a central body. Given this background, various models for the structure of the proposed autonomous Lutheran Church–Canada were considered.

One novel structure, proposed as early as 1979, was to divide the Church into three geographic areas. Each area would be comprised of three or four circuits with each circuit comprised of about twenty-five congregations. Circuits would meet four times a year to deal with recommendations from congregations, each of which would be represented by a pastor and a lay member. The circuits would have the officers typical of organizations chosen in various ways. They would also present nominees to the church body for area vice-president, who would be full-time parish pastors with vicars, whose responsibility it would be to assist the church body president in spiritual care and nurture of area congregations and church workers.

In this structure, the church body would meet twice a year to deal with recommendations from circuits, each of which would have three representatives. The national church body would also have officers, some of whom would serve as the Board of Directors. They and the program executives would serve as full-time staff. There would not be any general conventions. Funds would flow from congregations to the church body through the circuits.[30]

---

30   Suggested structure sketched by Herbert Mueller for the meeting of a special committee of Lutheran Church–Canada early in 1979.

Eventually, all efforts to form a novel structure were rejected and the entire structure of the Missouri Synod was adopted. The only changes proposed were those which substituted Canadian counterparts for American references in the bylaws of the Synod.

**

The most difficult and controversial issue facing the Ways and Means Committee related to pastoral training. In November 1976, the synodically-approved, fledgling branch-seminary in St. Catharines had been incorporated under the laws of the Province of Ontario. Ownership was vested in a group of twenty Missouri Synod Canadians elected by the District. This group named three laymen, three pastors, and the District President as its Board of Directors. Its program was accredited as an extension of the Synod's Fort Wayne seminary. By 1979, however, the Synod had become aware that the St. Catharines program was jeopardizing the accreditation of the Fort Wayne seminary itself. To address the situation, the Synod voted to give independent status to the St. Catharines program. To provide accreditation for its program, the seminary negotiated an affiliated status with nearby Brock University. At the same time, it also negotiated to lease land on the university campus upon which to build a permanent seminary building.

The same convention that approved independent status for the program in St. Catharines in 1979 also voted to phase out the temporary pastoral training arrangement in Saskatoon in which fifteen Missouri Synod students were enrolled at the time. The convention asked Synod's Board for Higher Education, in consultation with the Canadian Districts, to implement a definite plan for transition of the program in Saskatoon to a satisfactory permanent arrangement prior to its next convention; the class entering in the fall of 1980 was to be the last to legitimately enter the Saskatoon program.

By these two convention actions, the Synod had signalled already in 1979 that it favoured having two seminaries in Canada: one in St. Catharines in the East and one in the West in an undetermined location. Some Canadians, however, felt another option to the two-seminary solution should be considered: a single, centrally located seminary, possibly in Winnipeg. Carl Wagner, echoing the concern of many other laymen in the Manitoba and Saskatchewan District, challenged the financial viability of two seminaries. "We will be hard pressed to adequately support one seminary," he wrote. "One well-staffed and equipped seminary is far superior to two mediocre operations." Wagner also felt that one seminary would help bridge the chasm in the church between East and West in Canada. "An east and west seminary clearly indicates a physical division among us," he wrote. "A centrally located seminary would save face for everyone." But, realizing his views were not generally supported, he sided with the views most favoured in his District: "If we must compromise on two seminaries, it appears in the short run that Saskatoon is the only viable option in the West."[31]

To deal with the difficult problem of seminary training, Lutheran Church–Canada established a Higher Education Committee at its convention in Regina in 1979. Its first task was to explore, along with the Synod's Board for Higher Education, the question of whether there should be one centralized seminary program or two separate programs. If it recommended two programs, it was also asked to explore where the Western seminary should be located.

31   Letter of Carl Wagner to R. Ballenthin, August 30, 1979.

Although the Synod had decided in 1979 to discontinue the Chair of Theology at the Saskatoon seminary, there were obvious economic benefits in maintaining a program using the facilities of the seminary in Saskatoon. Thus, a committee of supporters from the Manitoba and Saskatchewan District developed a "Project Design for Missouri Synod training in Saskatoon" in 1980. Building on earlier studies of options for providing theological education in Canada, the committee proposed creating a new, permanent, independent and parallel seminary which would share the facilities of the Saskatoon seminary but would have its own program and board. Promoted as a seminary within a seminary, it was labelled Concordia House.

The whole seminary matter was brought for a final resolution to the 1981 convention of the Synod. After a lively debate at the Synod convention, the delegates referred the whole matter to Lutheran Church–Canada to decide in a "fair and consistent manner." Recognizing that there were only fourteen voting delegates at a convention of Lutheran Church–Canada as constituted at the time, the Board of Directors of Lutheran Church–Canada first convened a conference which brought together one hundred and forty representatives from across Canada to provide broader input to this very crucial issue. Only after this larger conference had discussed the seminary issue, was the Lutheran Church–Canada convention convened in Winnipeg on November 18-20, 1981. Based on the input from the conference, the convention voted for the two seminary programs. It subsequently also chose Edmonton as the location of the Western program.

In spite of this decision, the supporters of a Saskatoon seminary continued to promote the Concordia House concept. Both Districts in Western Canada were divided on the question and, by a narrow margin, both 1982 conventions asked that the establishment of the Edmonton seminary be deferred until Lutheran Church–Canada had become autonomous. They also asked in the meantime that involvement in Saskatoon be extended.

However, since the Synod had given Lutheran Church–Canada the authority to decide the issue and Lutheran Church–Canada had done so at a properly constituted convention, the Synod's Board for Higher Education and the Higher Education Committee of Lutheran Church–Canada, which the Synod's Board had begun to phase into the operation of its institutions in Canada, regarded the matter as settled.

The Committee took the first step of establishing a Task Force, chaired by retired university professor Albert Riep, to detail how a seminary could be established in Edmonton. Also serving on the Task Force were the five members of the Higher Education Committee and the presidents of the two western Districts: Roy Holm and Ed Lehman.

The two Canadian seminaries were thus both recognized as institutions of the Missouri Synod and when Lutheran Church–Canada became autonomous they would become institutions of the new church, functioning legally according to its constitution. In the meantime, the Synodical Board authorized the Board of Directors of Lutheran Church–Canada to appoint an interim Board of Regents for the seminary in St. Catharines. To accommodate the fact that incorporation under the Province of Ontario made the St. Catharines seminary responsible to a Board of Directors, the members of that Board of Directors were appointed as the Synod's Interim Board of Regents.

Meanwhile, the Edmonton seminary had officially come into being though a Private Member's Bill to the Alberta Legislature, and the Board of Directors of Lutheran Church–Canada also appointed its interim Board of Regents in July 1983.

***

With the seminary question settled, the two programs were able to proceed appropriately to carry out their function of preparing pastors for the church. In 1980, a year after the Ontario District celebrated its centennial, the St. Catharines seminary graduated its first five graduates. They included Thomas Pracher who would later serve as the President of the Central District. They would be followed in successive years by a steady stream of graduates who would go forth to serve the church, not only in Canada but also in the United States. When the seminary became an affiliated college of Brock University in 1982, most of its graduates were granted a Master of Divinity degree from the University.

In Edmonton, action was taken to implement plans for the seminary program to begin in the fall of 1984. An Edmonton-based site committee had recommended that the seminary should be located in the former president's house on the campus of Concordia College for at least the first three years. The house had been renovated for use by the seminary and the two institutions could share recreational facilities and activities, food services, and some library resources. The students could benefit from joint chapel services and other associations. Some academic programs, such as Greek courses at the College, would also be available to the seminary students.

In September 1983, the Seminary's Board of Regents met and called Ted Janzow as the founding president of the seminary. Janzow came with impeccable credentials, having served for fourteen years as the president of Concordia Teachers' College in Seward,

Nebraska. Although he had never served the church in Canada, he was known to many of the pastors in Western Canada. He had served as a District convention essayist. And his father and two of his uncles had served as pioneer pastors in the two Districts. Serving as Academic Dean and Dean of Students respectively were Ronald Vahl and Norman Threinen, both of whom earned Doctor of Theology degrees from Concordia Seminary in St. Louis. Two students had begun their studies under the Saskatoon program; two others had completed a year of seminary study in St. Louis; and the entire first year student body had been recruited by Janzow in the months prior to the opening of the seminary in September 1984. In spite of initial scepticism about the small seminary's viability, the two Districts in Western Canada showed that they accepted the seminary when, two years later, they passed resolutions thanking God for His gift of the seminary and pledging the Districts' wholehearted continuing support of it.

A study committee of Lutheran Church–Canada had earlier expressed the view in 1967 that a Canadian program was essential because "clergy must be acquainted with, and to some extent identify with, the history and culture of the people they serve and hope to win." To a great extent, this general description also applied to the seminaries serving Lutheranism in Canada.

Although both seminaries were intended to serve the Synod and subsequently Lutheran Church–Canada, the St. Catharines program reflected the culture and tendencies of Lutherans in Ontario and the Edmonton program reflected the culture and tendencies of Lutherans in the West. St. Catharines also tended to display many of the characteristics of the Missouri Synod's Fort Wayne seminary which had spawned it: more highly liturgical and leaning in the direction of the Wilhelm Loehe tradition of church and ministry. Edmonton tended to display many of the characteristics of the Synod's St. Louis seminary upon whose curriculum its program was patterned: it was somewhat more evangelical and leaning in the direction of the C. F. W. Walther tradition of church and ministry. While not anticipating that the two seminaries would be carbon copies of each other, they both faced the major challenge of recognizing each other as colleagues who had the responsibility together of serving an autonomous Lutheran Church–Canada in years to come.

***

An important part of the story of the movement of Lutheran Church–Canada toward an autonomous church pertained to the Canadian part of the Synod-wide Forward in Remembrance Thankoffering. On November 19, 1979, the Board of Directors of Lutheran Church–Canada met with the Synod's Director of the special offering to prepare a Mission and Ministry Statement for the Canadian portion of the offering. A challenging goal was set at $750,000 for World Missions; $750,000 for Training of an Indigenous Ministry; and $500,000 for Home Missions in Canada. But by June 1981, the pledges from the Canadian Church had more than doubled its goal of Two Million Dollars. In June 1982, the Board of Directors adopted as its World Missions project—for which it allocated US$175,000—the building of a seminary for the Lutheran Church in Korea.

In contrast to previous projections which had always assumed that an autonomous Lutheran Church–Canada would be financially dependent on the Missouri Synod, the success of this Thankoffering in Canada showed that this need not be the case. In September 1983, the three Canadian Districts could report that each was financially independent, that they were allocating $1,500,000 to home missions and, in addition, had raised a total of $4,365,131 from their midst through Forward in Remembrance.

The seminaries were the major beneficiary of the success of Forward in Remembrance: the St. Catharines seminary received $500,000 toward the building of its new seminary on the campus of Brock University and the Edmonton seminary was allocated $75,000 for the first year's operating costs and the cost of three years' rent of the renovated president's house.

This positive financial picture continued to be the case as the Missouri Synod conducted another special offering five years later entitled Alive in Christ. Canadians again participated and by February 1988 had raised another $1,279,425.

***

Encouraged by the successes they were experiencing, the delegates to the Lutheran Church–Canada convention in November 1981 re-elected Treit as president. Other officers elected were: Holm as vice-president; Lehman as secretary; Bill Buller, a layman from Windsor, as treasurer; Stanfel and Walt Seehagel, a layman from Calgary, as members-at-large. At this convention, the Ways and Means Committee was officially dissolved, with the Higher Education subcommittee continued as a Committee on Higher Education of Lutheran Church–Canada.

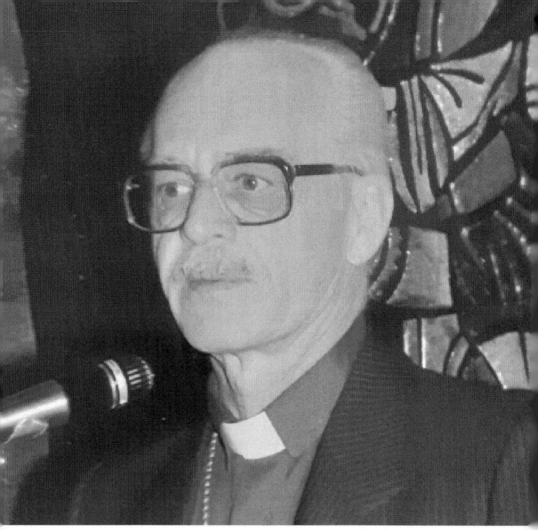

Rev. Elroy Treit, LCC F President 1977 to 1988.
He saw LCC F through to LCC in 1988.

CHAPTER 10
The Goal in Sight

T he Synod in convention in 1979 had adopted a formal resolution encouraging "Lutheran Church–Canada to proceed with the formation of a self-governing, indigenous Lutheran Church–Canada." The 1982 conventions of the three

Canadian geographical Districts also encouraged Lutheran Church–Canada to continue its efforts toward the formation of an autonomous Canadian church.

In its convention in 1983, the Synod approved in principle a series of procedures which could culminate in Lutheran Church–Canada becoming operative as an autonomous partner church as early as January 1, 1987. The schedule adopted by the Synod as a guide in 1983 was as follows:

• The Missouri Synod expresses its willingness to dissolve its Canadian Districts upon completion of the plans for the formation of Lutheran Church–Canada;

• Prior to April 1985, Lutheran Church–Canada conducts congregational information presentations;

• The Districts by a simple majority vote in each of the three geographic Districts approve the constitution and bylaws; each District by a simple majority requests dissolution by the Synod;

• In Fall 1985, Lutheran Church–Canada in convention deals with any remaining questions in preparation for a congregational vote;

• In 1986 prior to January 21, individual congregations are given the opportunity to vote whether or not they wish to join the autonomous Lutheran Church–Canada;

• In July 1986, if preceding actions are favourable, the Missouri Synod gives final approval for the establishment of an autonomous Lutheran Church–Canada as a partner church with the Missouri Synod;

• In Fall 1986, Lutheran Church–Canada holds a constituting convention.

***

The initial step to prepare for autonomy involved the preparation of a constitution and bylaws for an autonomous Church in Canada to replace the one under which the federation of the three Canadian Districts had been functioning. After this new constitution was shared with and approved by the Missouri Synod congregations in Canada, each of the Districts expressed itself in favour of the establishment of an autonomous Lutheran Church–Canada and urged congregations and their members with objections or concerns to forward them to the Board of Directors of the District so the 1985 convention of Lutheran Church–Canada could make whatever further adjustments were necessary.

After the proposed constitution and bylaws had been approved by the congregations and the Districts, it was reviewed by the Synod's Commission on Constitutional Matters, Commission on Theology and Church Relations, the Board for Mission Services and the Board of Directors.

To provide congregations in Canada with the information needed to vote intelligently regarding their possible participation in an autonomous Lutheran Church–Canada, the Board of Directors appointed an ad hoc committee to prepare four brochures along with an audio-visual presentation. Entitled: "What's This—A New Lutheran Church?"; "Leaving Missouri Synod?"; "Committed to Ministry!"; and "It's Up to You!" these brochures became the basis for a series of meetings across the country where information was communicated and discussed on the congregational level.

As a result of several meetings with Synodical Officers of the Missouri Synod, the Board of Directors of Lutheran Church–Canada also created a document entitled: "Formation of Lutheran Church–Canada as an Autonomous Partner Church with The Lutheran

Church—Missouri Synod" for distribution to all congregations in Canada in preparation for the District Conventions in 1985.

In a 1984 memorandum, the Secretary of the Synod assessed the Canadian scene as it moved toward autonomy. "It is clear that the District Presidents are committed to the formation of LCC as a partner church," he wrote. But he also detected "strong opposition on the part of a significant number of pastors and congregations [in Ontario]." The concern of many pastors related to "transfer and mobility." The concern of congregations focused on the west as "liberal." "Basically, I believe they desire autonomy," he wrote. "But they are hesitant to give up the security which they feel they have as members of LCMS." He continued: "It is reflected in frequent references to a 'transition period' and 'grace period,' and similar phrases when discussing the matters of pastoral transfer, independent congregation decisions, etc."[32] His assessment echoed many of the concerns which had been voiced over the years as Lutheran Church–Canada had struggled to move toward an autonomous church in Canada.

It was a concern confirmed by letters which the officers of Lutheran Church–Canada also received. For example, a pastor in London wrote to Ed Lehman, as the Secretary of the Board of Directors, in February 1985. Although the writer admitted he was basically opposed to the notion of Lutheran Church–Canada autonomy, he wrote he was disturbed that the suggested timetable to autonomy, which sounded so flexible in the 1983 Proceedings of the Synod, had become more of a target than a suggestion. He felt that French-speaking pastors were very much in the dark about what was at stake for them before being forced into a convention vote on the

---

32   Walter Rosin to Ralph A Bohlman, July 6, 1984.

matter. He was unclear as to what would become of congregations who aren't interested in autonomy and what the exact status will be of pastors who may remain in Canada for now but who wish to continue on the roster of Synod. "The impression that is coming out to us," he wrote, "is that objective [autonomy] has been pre-determined and it is going to be pushed right on through whether the grass roots of the church has the specific information it deserves or not." "That," he felt, "could lead to a very unpleasant scenario at the Ontario District convention in June and to deeply ruptured feelings between East and West even if LCC does become a reality."[33]

As the time for congregations and pastors to cast a vote regarding their participation in an autonomous Lutheran Church–Canada in the fall of 1985 drew nearer, Mervin Huras, Assistant to President Al Stanfel, who was convalescing in the hospital at the time, convened a "free conference" for people to unburden themselves. About fifty people attended, representing themselves and, in some cases, congregations. Huras reported that most of them were opponents to autonomy for Lutheran Church–Canada.

Some of the concerns of people who attended the conference focused on the financing of Lutheran Church–Canada. Others felt both the study and the numbers were inadequate and that costs would be much higher than indicated. Still others were concerned that the two western districts would out-vote the east and that creeping liberalism from the western Districts would affect the church body. It was generally recognized that, while the proposed constitution follows the Missouri Synod Constitution, it might be too top heavy and costly for Canada. There was concern whether Lutheran

---

33   Robert Bugbee to Edwin Lehman, February 4, 1985.

Church–Canada could be involved in a meaningful way in world missions. While the general direction of the conference was basically negative, some participants did indicate they would support an autonomous Lutheran Church–Canada if their concerns were met prior to the convention.[34]

In spite of the negative vibrations from Ontario congregations and pastors reported to the Board of Directors, the delegates to the Lutheran Church–Canada convention in November 6-10, 1985, passed a resolution with a 95 percent majority vote to continue steps toward the establishment of an autonomous church body. Three issues had come to the attention of the Board of Directors which needed further attention: the need for a detailed plan of mission outreach, including French ministry; the need for more detailed financial projections; and the desire for revisions to "The Memorandum of Agreement" which would form the basis of the protocol agreement between Lutheran Church–Canada and The Lutheran Church—Missouri Synod. The final concern centered on matters such as the process by which pastors could transfer back and forth between the two bodies, the portability of pension plans for full-time church workers, and so forth. The Board attempted to provide summary answers to these concerns in a final printed document entitled: "In Him We Live, On the Road to Autonomy" and through personal information provided by the Board of Directors.

**

By January 16, 1986, each congregation and pastor in a Missouri Synod congregation in Canada had the opportunity to vote whether they intended to participate in an autonomous Lutheran Church–

---

34   John Schuelke to Walter Rosin, October 25, 1985.

Canada. Ballots were distributed to be marked "Yes" or "No." The results of the balloting reported by Treit were as follows:

	CONGREGATIONS	CLERGY
Alberta - British Columbia District	*108 yes (1 no)*	*102 yes (1 no)*
Manitoba & Saskatchewan District	*76 yes (6 no)*	*52 yes (3 no)*
Ontario District	*52 yes (26 no)*	*40 yes (35 no)*
Minnesota-North (Non-Geographical District)	*14 yes (2 no)*	*7 yes (1 no)*
Total	*250 yes (35 no)*	*201 yes (50 no)*

In the communiqué accompanying the report on the balloting, Treit stated that he felt "very happy" with the results. "All in all, with 87% across the country for congregations and 66% in Ontario, it is the feeling of the Board and myself personally that we are on the way," wrote Treit. He stated that he was not surprised that such a large number of pastors in the Ontario District voted "no." He reasoned that, "of the 35 [pastors] that voted 'no,' we have twenty-six Americans who still have some very strong ties to the close U.S. Districts." He claimed, however, that there were eight pastors who had told him personally that, if the vote was positive, they would get on the 'bandwagon' and get the job done.[35]

While Stanfel fully agreed with autonomy, his interpretation of

---

35   Elroy Treit, attachment to a letter to Walter Rosin, March 3, 1986.

the results of the Ontario vote was quite different from Treit's. When asked, "What, if anything, would be done in the way of following up on the negative concerns" voiced by participants at the free conference, Stanfel indicated he had discussed the matter with Treit, who felt nothing needed to be done. But Stanfel was concerned because some good, strong, healthy congregations were involved in this move—congregations that were doctrinally sound and heavy supporters of the Missouri Synod. "They are needed to make Lutheran Church–Canada a success," Stanfel maintained, "and leadership should bend over backwards to help them and try to meet with them prior to the [1986 Synodical] convention."

At any event, the balloting in 1986 clearly stated that some pastors and congregations who were currently members of a geographical Canadian Districts of the Synod would choose not to become part of the autonomous Lutheran Church–Canada. What was to happen to these pastors and congregations when the new church was constituted?

In the Memorandum of Agreement adopted by the 1985 convention of Lutheran Church–Canada and the Board of Directors of the Missouri Synod (summarized in "In Him We Live On The Road to Autonomy") gave the following answer: "Members who do not elect to join Lutheran Church–Canada are reminded of the right to become independent... If they become independent, Lutheran Church–Canada and The Lutheran Church—Missouri Synod will make every effort to provide service to them, as desired, through an arrangement with existing Districts..." The Missouri Synod clearly indicated it would not function indefinitely in Canada, but adequate time would be given both by Lutheran Church–Canada and the Missouri Synod for congregations to consider their eventual membership in Lutheran Church–Canada while being served and remaining members of the Missouri Synod in the meantime.

Among the pastors and congregations invited to vote on participating in an autonomous Lutheran Church–Canada were a number located in Northwestern Ontario which had hitherto been part of the Minnesota North District of the Missouri Synod.[36] Together with the two Districts in Western Canada, they overwhelmingly voted their intention to become part of an autonomous Lutheran Church–Canada.

***

The Slovak Evangelical Lutheran Church (SELC) and English Districts of the Missouri Synod in Canada had also been invited to participate in the vote on an autonomous church. The SELC District, which had ten congregations in Canada in 1983, had only minimal involvement in the story of the developing Lutheran Church–Canada over the years. Since it had only recently become a District of the Missouri Synod and had not even found its identity within the Synod, its leadership thought it was too soon for its Canadian congregations to make another switch. Thus, they had requested they not be involved in the balloting.

The English District also had ten congregations in Canada in 1983. Representatives of the District had been involved with the development of Lutheran Church–Canada right from the beginning in 1956. The Canadian Council of the English District had requested in 1961 that English District congregations located in Canada be eligible for membership in Lutheran Church–Canada while remaining affiliated with the English District. But the delegates to the 1961 convention had made it clear that the new autonomous church would

---

36   For the story of this development see Norman J. Threinen, *A Sower Went Out, Supplement:* 21-30, 37-57.

not have non-geographic Districts. While three congregations voted in favour of forming an autonomous Canadian Church in the referendum in 1964, all of them abstained from voting in 1986.

***

The Missouri Synod convention in Indianapolis in 1986 was a crucial point in the development of Lutheran Church–Canada as an indigenous church body in Canada. It was this convention which was to provide for a constituting convention for the autonomous Lutheran Church–Canada in the fall of 1986. However, a large number of pastors and congregations in the Ontario District were not prepared to become part of an autonomous Lutheran Church–Canada under the present circumstances. They thus sent a message to the Board of Directors that there were some very important issues relative to the mission of Lutheran Church–Canada which needed to be addressed before the church in Canada could take the step of autonomy and partnership with the Synod.

On July 20, 1986, a number of delegates to the Synod convention met with members of the Board of Directors of Lutheran Church–Canada about the concerns of pastors and congregations which had voted "no" on the balloting. Having identified the concerns, an informal polling of Ontario District pastors at the convention indicated that an overwhelming number were in favour of a substitute motion which would ask the Synod to postpone for one year the calling for a constituting convention in 1986 to permit time to address the concerns.

Recognizing the validity of the concerns raised and anxious to address them if possible, the Executive Committee of Lutheran Church–Canada asked the Missouri Synod to delay by one year the calling of the constituting convention. The delay would permit additional time to consult and cooperate with the Districts in the development of a realistic and comprehensive home missions strategy, including goals, objectives, specific mission sites, and specialized training of mission personnel; to undertake intensive consultation with French language mission workers; to establish procedures and to allocate funds to facilitate the advanced theological training of Canadians for leadership and professorial positions; to listen to and consider all suggestions and concerns from pastors and congregations regarding the future of Lutheran Church–Canada; to reiterate its commitment to the ongoing operation of two seminaries in Canada; to distribute the Protocol Document between Lutheran Church–Canada and the Synod well in advance of final acceptance of such a document so that both individuals and congregations would have ample opportunity for input to the Board of Directors; and to implement the decision to encourage the three Canadian geographical Districts to begin channelling more of their "at large" support to Lutheran Church–Canada in order to adequately finance the goals and gradually assemble a national staff.[37]

Satisfied that the Executive Committee had heard their concerns and were committed to addressing them, the Ontario District delegation pledged themselves to return to Ontario with the resolve to do all in their power under the blessing of God to encourage all of the pastors and congregations of the Missouri Synod there to participate in the establishment of an autonomous Lutheran Church–Canada.

Subsequently, a convention floor committee which had all three of the Canadian District presidents on it, including Roger Winger who

_____

37   Minutes, Lutheran Church–Canada Board of Directors (Executive Committee), Indianapolis, Indiana, July 21, 1986.

had succeeded Stanfel as president, brought to the convention of the Missouri Synod resolution R-85-01-03: "To Authorize the Board of Directors of Lutheran Church–Canada to delay the dates for the Constituting Convention and Autonomy." The resolution resolved "that the Board of Directors of Lutheran Church–Canada be encouraged to defer the constituting convention to a date that falls within the first six months of 1987; and that the effective date of autonomy be not less than three months after the constituting convention."

Bill Ney, the pastor of Redeemer, Waterloo, who had largely served as the spokesman for the concerned pastors from Ontario at the convention in Indianapolis, later wrote to ABC District President Ed Lehman: "I have spoken personally with a couple of the primary opponents of LCC in Ontario and am gratified to discover a new, positive mood and an openness and willingness to reconsider their position." He cited a case of one pastor, whose congregation had asked for time on the agenda of the Board of Directors of the Synod's Michigan District, who informed him his congregation had cancelled its request and put it 'on hold indefinitely.' Ney wrote: "I can assure you that Pastors and Congregations see their concerns seriously addressed by the LCC Board and its Committees, I am convinced they will join us in LCC in June 1988.[38]

***

Aside from the above-mentioned pastors and congregations, some who were attracted to being in a Canadian church body and were proud to be Canadians decided for various reasons not to be part of an independent Lutheran Church–Canada. Most of them were the pastors and congregations of the English District in Ontario

---

38   Ney to Lehman, July 30, 1986.

which were primarily urban, cosmopolitan, flexible with regard to altar fellowship, and open to relationships with other Christians using cutting edge mission methods.[39] The planners of the autonomous Lutheran Church–Canada took the approach that, although it was desirable for purposes of national identity or for legal reasons for these pastors and congregations to join Lutheran Church–Canada, the time period for doing so was not critical. Their non-geographical nature allowed for a gradual transition.

Also included in the group who decided not to become part of an independent Lutheran Church–Canada were three pastors and congregations which had been members of the Ontario District. Among them was Louis Scholl and his congregation in Windsor. The approach of the planners of the autonomous Lutheran Church–Canada to these pastors and congregations was to remind them they had the right to become independent or to apply for membership in a District of the Missouri Synod. It was felt desirable, above all, that their mission and ministry should not be hindered but that they be supported and encouraged to carry it out as effectively as possible. These three congregations, along with a fourth which had existed as an independent congregation and had been served by Missouri Synod pastors for about a century, elected to remain with the Synod by joining the English District.[40]

***

On October 3-5, 1986, a pensive Elroy Treit met with his Board of Directors. He looked at the prospect that he would soon be relinquishing his position as president of Lutheran Church–Canada. His diabetes had progressed to the point where it was having a debilitating

---

39   Based on an e-mail to the author, January 23, 2019.
40   *In Him We Live On the Road to Autonomy*, 6.

and deteriorating effect on his health. It had affected his feet and had begun to affect his hands and fingers. Under no circumstances could he consider serving as the president of the autonomous Lutheran Church–Canada. "As of the last couple of months, I have had a feeling that I just cannot shake," Treit said. "It was the same feeling that Alexander the Great had after he had conquered the then known world. He wept because, as he said, 'There are no more worlds to conquer.' That was his goal and he had accomplished it."

"I had a goal in 1977," said Treit. "In the naive view of a forty-four year-old stripling youth, I felt that the job could be done in four to six years, tops! As we now know, the goal will come to completion in essence sometime in May of 1988, God willing. The emotional experience of the 1986 Synodical convention, the unanimous vote, the singing of our national anthem, the expression of thanks from various people and the future loss of precious fellowship with classmates and others in the Missouri Synod was that once in an era, or once in time, historical event. I learned too, that it meant much to the American members of the Missouri Synod and they too were just beginning to see the impact of the resolution on their own lives in the church.

"I say these things," continued Treit, "because I want you to understand that I had accepted the position and the attendant responsibilities because I had a singleness of purpose in mind; that of bringing a group of people into a position of self-responsibility, self-governance, hopefully changing a myopic view of membership and purpose into a challenge of new-found zeal and a wider vision of the Great Commission. As I did this, I did it according to the dictates of my own conscience, and in a manner and style that was uniquely mine.... Throughout the years, I have not viewed this office as the ego gratification for a spotlight in national or international ecclesiastical politics. I had made a promise to myself—after, I might add, a lot of hours spent in prayer—that this was a God-given duty, nothing more, and so I did it my way. And for better or for worse, the legacy is nearing its completion."

***

In October 1986, a draft copy of the protocol document between Lutheran Church–Canada and the Missouri Synod was shared with congregations and pastors across Canada. It included paragraphs on the basis, the goal, and the objectives of the partnership between the two bodies. It also contained declarations or agreements on the following subjects: mutual altar and pulpit fellowship, fellowship with other church bodies, membership consisting of congregations, pastors and commissioned ministers, common participation in certain meetings, auxiliaries and other organizations, assets and liabilities, assignment of corporate entities, cooperative efforts under operating agreements, solicitation of funds, and provision for amendments to the protocol document.

In May 1987, an All-Canada conference of church workers was held. Church workers from across the country met in Winnipeg to strengthen the bond of Canadian Lutherans. In June 26-27, 1987, the Board of Directors received an eleven-page document entitled: "Masterplan for Mission: An Outline for the Mission of Lutheran Church–Canada to the year AD 2000." At the end of 1987, the Board of Directors adopted a spending budget of $1,179,900 with receipts of $1,179,000 for 1988.

The founding convention of the autonomous Lutheran Church–

Canada was held in Winnipeg from May 18-21, 1988, with an effective start date of January 1, 1988. In preparation for the new church, Treasurer Bill Buller had been hired as the Executive Director on April 6, 1986. While Treit continued to develop agendas for Board meetings, Buller was responsible for soliciting reports of the various committees for the Board, thus relieving Treit of much of the work. Buller was also the convention manager for the founding convention of Lutheran Church–Canada. What had been a dream for many years became a reality in May of 1988.

PART 2

FROM AUTONOMY ONWARD

1987-1996

LUTHERAN CHURCH–CANADA

Edwin Lehman

PRELUDE

The vision of an autonomous Canadian Lutheran Church in fellowship with The Lutheran Church—Missouri Synod was now over forty years old. With every change of leadership, new hopes were kindled, and, in most cases, new target dates were set by which an autonomous church would become a reality.

By the end of 1985, thanks to the determined leadership of Lutheran Church–Canada's president, Rev. Elroy Treit, and the tireless efforts of the Board of Directors and the Ways and Means Committee, most of the difficult issues had been resolved. Two seminaries were now preparing pastors for the Canadian church, one in St. Catharines, Ontario and one in Edmonton. The theological education program at Luther Theological Seminary in Saskatoon, not without its blessings nor its deficiencies, had been phased out. A draft constitution for the new synod was in its final stages.

President Treit had held several meetings with LCMS president Ralph Bohlmann and had drafted a "Protocol Agreement" which was widely shared with the constituency. Policies were developed to facilitate the movement of pastors, seminary graduates, and other church workers between the two churches. Agreements were reached for transitioning workers from LCMS worker benefit plans to those of LCC. Any misgivings about the ability of a Canadian church to be financially self-supporting were allayed as a result of the overwhelming response to the Synod-wide appeal, "Forward in Remembrance." Each of the Canadian districts exceeded their suggested goals by a wide margin.[1]

With the dissolution of the Joint Commission on Inter-Lutheran Relationships in 1979, a three-way merger of Lutherans in Canada was no longer on the table. The Lutheran Church in America - Canada Section and the Evangelical Lutheran Church of Canada eventually merged to form the new Evangelical Lutheran Church in Canada at a constituting convention in May 1985. It seemed that the final seconds on the clock were ticking down. The long-sought dream would soon become a reality. Or would there be a last-minute glitch?

At its 1986 convention in Indianapolis, Indiana, the Missouri Synod was prepared to pass a resolution giving its blessing to the formation of the new Canadian church, with a constituting convention to be held that fall. Before debate on the resolution began, it became apparent that a small but determined number of Canadian

---

1   Of the thirty-eight LCMS districts, the Manitoba and Saskatchewan district was the second highest in exceeding its goal.

delegates were prepared to speak against it. The last thing we needed was to show the 1,000 plus American delegates how deeply divided the 45 Canadian delegates were! What to do? The decision was made to hold an emergency caucus of all Canadian delegates that evening to deal with a potentially embarrassing situation.

It became evident that those opposed were not categorically against the concept of an autonomous church. They just felt that they were not yet ready. There were too many intangibles that left them uncomfortable. In response to those concerns, members of the LCC Board of Directors who were present as delegates, proposed a further postponement of the founding convention to the spring of 1988, leaving the coming year (1987) free for an all-Canada church workers' conference, specifically focused on any outstanding issues.

Those who had earlier indicated they would speak against the motion agreed that this would satisfy their concerns, on the condition that the proposal to hold the All-Canada Conference, along with its intended purpose of addressing any and all outstanding issues, would be presented to the convention along with the resolution. As a result, when the motion came to the floor the next day, only one Canadian delegate (who had not attended the previous evening's caucus) spoke against the motion.

And thus, the resolution passed, with a May 1988 date for a constituting convention, and a January 1, 1989 date for the legal beginning of the autonomous church.

The Board of Directors of the federation had actually discussed the concept of an all-Canada church workers conference long before it was mentioned in Indianapolis, but had not made a final decision. Now the board acted swiftly to make the necessary arrangements.

With progress towards autonomy requiring more and more time from members of the board, especially from President Elroy Treit, who also served a large and active congregation in Vancouver, the decision had been made to engage LCC's first full-time staff member. On April 6, 1986, Bill Buller, who, as a member of the Board of Directors also served as the federation's treasurer, was engaged to serve full-time as the federation's executive director. Now, all his attention was on making arrangements for the All-Canada Conference, scheduled for May 14-17, 1987.

The sense of the board was that the outstanding issues were not related to any of the major decisions already made but rather to some of the intangibles. One of these was the need for assurance that we shared a common theological position, especially between east and west. This had been a lingering concern due to the very limited interaction most of the pastors from eastern Canada had with those of the west, and vice-versa. This was quite understandable; even with conventions of the federation every two or three years, there were never more than about 40 delegates present. Also, while pastors freely accepted calls between the two western districts, most calls in and out of the Ontario District were with neighbouring American districts. Most of those attending the conference would, therefore, be meeting each other for the first time.

There was also a concern regarding the ability of the new church to undertake a serious mission program, even though this was a matter to which the Missions subcommittee of the Ways and Means Committee had already given a great deal of attention.

Finally, although this matter was not publicly raised, there was a sense that we had to assure those present that the new church's

Worker Benefit Plans would be at least as good as, or better than, the ones offered within the LCMS.

All-Canada Church Workers' Conference
May 14-17, 1987

When engineers are tasked with designing a new bridge, they know exactly what steps they will have to take. Ultimately, it's all about numbers. But when the church tries to bridge the differences between two (or more) groups of people, it's not that easy. Of course, how a meeting is structured, what agenda is followed, and so forth, are all important. But the successful outcome of such an effort is ultimately up to the Holy Spirit. The agenda for the All-Canada Church Workers' Conference was carefully structured to provide for a maximum amount of formal and informal interaction. At the same time, it was open-ended in the sense that there was no pressure to convince those who had some reservations, nor would there be any votes to test the level of agreement on any topics under discussion.

In addition to providing frequent opportunities for worship and Bible study, the conference heard major presentations by Dr. Ralph Bohlmann, president of LCMS, and seminary presidents Dr. Howard Kramer of St. Catharines and Dr. Ted Janzow of Edmonton. These were followed by small group discussions on various theological and practical issues. Other presentations dealt with Missions and Pension Plans. At its conclusion, all agreed that this conference not only answered many outstanding questions, but also provided excellent opportunities for interaction among the pastors, in many cases for the first time. Most important of all was the fact that some essential bridges, especially between east and west, had been built. Our prayers had been answered.

The All-Canada Conference was not only instrumental in putting to rest any lingering questions about an autonomous church, but it also accomplished something else. It was, in effect, a trial run for holding the Constituting Convention twelve months later. Although that convention would have more than double the attendance, from the standpoint of logistics this conference demonstrated that, for the most part, the plans being laid for the Constituting Convention were on the right track.

Constituting Convention
May 18-21, 1988

Twelve months later, it all came to pass. From Vancouver Island to New Brunswick, pastors and lay delegates from all 325 congregations, with only a handful of exceptions, gathered in Winnipeg's Convention Centre. They were joined by pastors not serving a congregation, including many retirees, parochial school teachers, and various other rostered workers, plus hundreds of visitors from within Canada, from the United States, and from around the world.

Minutes of meetings are usually a straight-forward account of what transpired. But the first paragraph of the minutes of the Constituting Convention's opening service reveal more than a little bit of excitement, as they record: "To the strains of 'All Hail the Power of Jesus' Name,' some 1,400 delegates, guests, and visitors raised their voices in worship and praise to open the Constituting Convention for the establishment of the autonomous Lutheran Church–Canada.

LCC Founding Convention 1988.

The service was held in the Convention Centre, Winnipeg, Manitoba, beginning on May 18, 1988 at 7:30 p.m. St. James Lutheran Church of Winnipeg served as the host congregation."

The anxiety and ambivalence that marked previous gatherings were nowhere evident. This time, it was not merely going to happen. It was actually happening. Only a few months shy of thirty years since the federation's first convention, an autonomous Lutheran Church–Canada was being born. Even those who had opposed it in the past were now ready to leave their reluctance behind, and to join in bringing about the best possible outcome by willingly serving in whatever way they could, and by supporting the actions which the new church was about to undertake.

The theme chosen for the convention was "Our Lord for Every Land." The words "Our Lord" recall the early church's confession, "Jesus is Lord," underscoring the importance of theology for the life of the church. The words "for Every Land" allude to the Great Commission as recorded in Matthew 28. The point of the convention theme, therefore, was that confessing the faith and sharing the faith (theology and missions) constitute a single mandate. They are not two competing options.

Because this was a constituting convention, and not just the restructuring of an existing body, a number of extraordinary resolutions were necessary before the assembly could move forward with the official formation of the autonomous synod. To that end, the Board of Directors had appointed a special committee headed by Dr. Norman Threinen to draft the necessary procedural resolutions. Chief among them was the enabling resolution which read, in part: "Resolved, that, with deep gratitude to God for His blessings on us and on our forebears, with loving appreciation to The Lutheran Church—Missouri Synod for nurturing and supporting the work in Canada for over 100 years, and with holy fear coupled with confidence in God's abiding grace, we, the delegates to this convention do hereby establish the Lutheran Church–Canada in the name of the Father and of the Son and of the Holy Spirit… Soli Deo Gloria!" The chair had scarcely called for a show of hands, when the assembly broke out in singing the Common Doxology.

But how does a federation of three districts, which is also an "administrative unit" of The Lutheran Church-Missouri Synod, become an autonomous body? The simplest way would have been for each of the three districts, in convention, to sever their affiliation with the LCMS and vote in favor of establishing Lutheran Church–Canada as an autonomous body. That would have been sufficient as far as the LCMS was concerned. But that would have meant that

LCC would always be considered a creation of the districts—in other words a federation.

The founding convention intentionally chose a different method, one that was more complicated but that upheld the concept of a synod created by its members (congregations, pastors, and other rostered workers). The synod, subsequently, would create three districts. This is the way the LCMS was created, and this is the way we wanted LCC to be formed.

The first resolution determined the official roster of Lutheran Church–Canada, an action which gave the delegates the authority to take the necessary steps for establishing the autonomous church. The final special resolution formalized the adoption of the constitution and bylaws of the new church. All voting delegates thereupon affixed their signatures to the constituting documents, beginning with the oldest and youngest pastoral delegates and the lay delegates representing the oldest and newest congregations from each district. Once all delegates had signed, any other lay or clergy members of LCC who wished to have their names recorded on the original copy of the constitution were invited to add their signatures.

With the constituting resolutions adopted, the delegates turned their attention to the election of the officers and directors of the new church. The results were as follows:

• President: Rev. Edwin Lehman (ABC)

• Vice Presidents: Rev. Karl Koslowsky (MS), Rev. Robert Bugbee (ON), and Rev. Orville Walz (ABC)

• Secretary: Rev. Roger Winger (ON)

• Treasurer: Mr. Ken Werschler (MS)

• Board of Directors: Rev. Karl Keller (ABC), Mr. John Fuge

(MS), Mr. Walter Heinemann(MS), Mr. Terry Morgan (ON), Mr. Alan Schmitt (ON), and Mr. Walter Seehagel (ABC).

The first chairman of the Board of Directors was Walter Seehagel. Partway into his first term, he and John Daniels were engaged to head up a new stewardship program. Since this could involve a conflict of interest, he resigned from the board and was replaced as chairman by Walter Heinemann. The vacant board position was filled with the appointment of Mr. Wm. Rusch (ABC).

International Guests

Because the three Canadian districts had been integral parts of The Lutheran Church—Missouri Synod for so many years, many synodical and district leaders were also present. Dr. Ralph Bohlmann, who had been elected president of the LCMS in 1981, presented appropriate plaques to President Treit and to the three Canadian District presidents, Revs. Stanfel, Holm, and Lehman. In addition he also presented a stained glass artwork depicting the logos of the LCMS and the new LCC on either side of the Luther seal. These were surrounded by symbols for the Lord's Supper, Baptism, the Bible, and the Holy Spirit. This art work has since been incorporated into the chapel of the synodical office in Winnipeg.

Other international guests included Johannes Gedrat from Brazil, Won Sang Ji from Korea, Allan Yung from Hong Kong, Arnold Rakow from England, Paul Kofi Fynn from Ghana, David Piso from Papua New Guinea, and Jobst Schoene from Germany.

At the conclusion of the founding convention, Bohlmann and Treit installed the new president, after which Lehman and Treit installed the other newly elected officers, along with board and committee members.

Stained glass depicting the logos of the LCMS and the new LCC on either side of the Luther seal, and surrounded by symbols for the Lord's Supper, Baptism, the Bible, and the Holy Spirit. Presented at the Constituting Convention by Dr. Ralph Bohlmann (President, LCMS 1981). Photo by David Friesen.

Subsequent Actions

Although the primary purpose of this convention was to officially launch the autonomous church, the delegates also passed a resolution stating the new synod's position on abortion. Delegates felt this was necessary, because around that time, the issue was being hotly debated in Canada's parliament, eventually leaving Canada without any legislation on abortion. LCC's resolution was based on what the Scriptures teach about the sanctify of life from the time of conception until natural death. It asked the president to send an appropriate letter reflecting our position to each member of Parliament. It was interesting to discover that a number of members from all parties agreed with the viewpoint our letter expressed—even though in subsequent years it became apparent that their personal views did not agree with that of their party.

When the convention adjourned, it was time for the three newly created districts to hold their conventions. Presidents Al Stanfel and Roy Holm were re-elected in the Ontario and Manitoba and Saskatchewan Districts, respectively. Rev. Harold Ruf was elected in the Alberta-British Columbia District to succeed Rev. Lehman.

Like the national body, the districts would also follow a three-year convention cycle. However, the national body agreed to hold its next convention in two years, rather than three. This was done for two reasons: first, to deal with any important issues that may not have been envisioned at the constituting convention, and secondly, to underscore the fact that since the national body had created the districts, it made sense that the districts would always meet in the year following the national convention.

Although the effective date on which the new LCC would become a legal corporation was set for January 1, 1989, most of the newly elected officers, boards, and committees began functioning immediately. Transfer of assets, launching a separate worker benefit plans, and the like, would take place on the January date.

To provide a proper observance of the 1989 launch, each congregation received a Proclamation, to be read to the assembled congregation on the first Sunday of the new year. The proclamation called upon all members of LCC "to humble themselves before God, confessing their sins and imploring His mercy in Jesus Christ... to lift up their hearts and voices, praising God for yesterday's blessings and tomorrow's opportunities... to recommit themselves to the regular hearing and reading of God's Word, and... to be fervent and frequent in prayer, eager and willing in their witness." In addition, every rostered worker and congregation received a certificate of membership in the autonomous LCC.

In preparation for the legal beginning of the new church, the pastors and congregations of the Ottawa circuit invited the president of LCC to be the guest preacher for an area wide service, held at St. Luke Lutheran Church in Ottawa on January 8, 1989. Civic, provincial, and national representatives were also invited, as were representatives of local and national media. For this occasion, Lehman preached on the words from Revelation 3:8—"Behold, I have set before you an open door."

Settling In

Since the new church now had three full-time staff members (Lehman, Werschler, and Buller[2]) and two support staff (Inge Schroeder and Erna Peppler), it was necessary to find a location for an office. For the first few months, we occupied a two room suite which Buller had rented on the second floor of the Courts of Saint James at 2727 Portage Avenue, in Winnipeg.

We quickly discovered an unexpected advantage in the fact that the three executive staff had their roots in each of the new church's three geographical districts. It meant that there was no congregation,

2   Buller's title was changed from "executive director" to "assistant to the president".

and virtually no pastor with which at least one member of the staff was not already acquainted.

Later that year, through the courtesy of Lutheran Church of the Redeemer, 59 Academy Road, we rented a larger area in their basement. This arrangement also meant we had space for meetings of the various boards and committees, eliminating the need to rent hotel space for such a purpose. When the time came to add a mission executive, plus additional support staff, another move was undertaken, this time to commercial office space at 200 Dublin Avenue, on the north side of the city.

President Edwin Lehman in front of new LCC Office Centre.

The present national office, at 3074 Portage Ave., was originally a commercial office building which LCC purchased and renovated. The renovation was carried out by volunteers from "Labourers for Christ." The project manager was LCC treasurer, Ken Werschler, while Bill McKee of Brandon, Manitoba served as engineer and August Zepick of Regina was the onsite foreman. The new facility was dedicated to the glory of God on June 18, 1995.

Throughout these early years, we experienced another unexpected blessing that we became aware of only in retrospect. Bill Buller and his wife Sarah had moved to Winnipeg about two years before the constituting convention and had rented an apartment in the Courts of Saint James. It was their common practice that whenever there was a meeting of the Board of Directors, they would invite all of us to their apartment for an evening meal. Having enjoyed Sarah's delicious cooking, we stayed for several hours afterwards and just got to know one another better. Then, instead of retiring to hotel rooms, we discovered that the Bullers had arranged for us to sleep in several of the guest rooms which the apartment complex had available for rent. These contained only two single beds, a dresser, and a washroom—no television or computer connections. Only later, did we discover Bill and Sarah had "method in their madness." If we had stayed in hotels, we would have eaten in a restaurant and then each gone to our rooms, usually sharing space with someone we already knew quite well. Since the sleeping quarters in the apartment complex were so Spartan, no one was in a hurry to retire to their room, and instead, the result was extended time for bonding as well as for informal conversation about the future of the new church.

Structural Issues

At its constituting convention, the new Lutheran Church–Canada adopted a document which was essentially an adaptation of the constitution and bylaws of The Lutheran Church—Missouri Synod. Why would a church body of some 325 congregations need a structure designed for a church body with more than 5,000 congregations? Would it not be too complicated for our purpose? Of course, but to adopt an original constitution proved to be more complicated than at first thought. With conventions of both the three districts and the federation held every three years it meant that if one district asked for amendments to a draft document, it could take at least three years, or possibly six years, for the revisions to be processed, due to the various convention cycles. And since all congregations, pastors, and other rostered workers were already living with the LCMS constitution, we decided we would simply adopt the 1983 version of the LCMS Constitution and Bylaws, adapted to the Canadian situation. This meant omitting references to LCMS seminaries, Concordia Publishing House, and some of the committees which LCC did not need.

Although the decision to base our constituting documents on those of the LCMS expedited the autonomy process, the disadvantages soon became apparent. Almost all of the major boards worked independently of one another. Staff members were responsible only to the board that called them. It meant that there were times when, before a certain project could be undertaken, it had to get approval from four or five separate boards or committees, and thus any one of them could kill the proposal. However inconvenient this arrangement was, it was not without its blessings. At least it forced all boards and committees, and more importantly the synodical staff, to be sensitive to how decisions made by one board can have an impact on decisions of other boards and committees.

It was always expected that major constitutional revisions would take place after autonomy. Attempts toward that end were on the agenda of every convention that followed, from 1990 on. The general response was either that it was too soon to do a major revision of the constitution and bylaws, or the proposals put forward were not acceptable to the grassroots. More substantial revisions, therefore, had to wait until after the election of Rev. Ralph Mayan, in 1996.

"Our Lord for Every Land"

The desire to share the Gospel with those in far-off lands was not the result of some new sense of identity as an autonomous church. Long before anyone had dreamed of an autonomous LCC, Canadian pastors, teachers, and laity had worked alongside their fellow LCMS members in virtually every continent on the globe. Some were salaried missionaries, many others volunteers. As far as can be determined, the first Canadian pastors to enter a foreign mission field did so in the early 1930s. These included Rev. Reinhold Schmidt,[3] who went to Argentina in 1932, and Rev. Albert Maschmeyer[4] who went to Brazil the same year. They were followed soon after by Rev. John Werschler[5] who also went to Brazil in 1933. At the time, the churches in South America were still districts of the LCMS. Canadian congregations loved to hear the stories of those who came home on

---

3   Information provided by Rev. Schmidt's son, Gerardo, of Fort Saskatchewan, Alberta.

4   Norman J. Threinen. *Like a Leaven*, 90.

5   Norman J. Threinen. *A Sower Went Out*, 84.

furloughs, and supported them with their generous offerings.

But now it would be different. Lutheran Church–Canada would assume responsibility for calling, sending, and supporting its own missionaries. We would learn to put into practice what we had already confessed, that our Lord was "for every land!"

Only in retrospect did we come to realize how God was already preparing the global harvest fields. In the years just before autonomy, and for a few years thereafter, there was an unprecedented interest in volunteer mission work, to a large extent involving young people. Some of these activities began under the auspices of the Missouri Synod, but mostly under the autonomous church. Our young people volunteered their services in Guatemala and in Papua New Guinea as teachers, in Japan as youth workers, in Hong Kong and Ukraine as evangelists, in Ghana as agriculturalists, in Cameroon as Bible Translators, and in South Africa to plant a new English-speaking congregation—in many cases, serving without remuneration. Some of the incentive for these activities was due to major changes in the way many countries had become more open to the Gospel. With the collapse of the Soviet Union, it was only a matter of time before the rest of eastern Europe would achieve independence. The collapse of the Berlin Wall in 1989 meant that the reunion of East and West Germany was inevitable. For a brief period of time in the early 1990s, the government of China openly supported the translation and publication of the Bible, and even allowed the establishment of a seminary in Nanjing for the training of indigenous pastors.

Since domestic mission outreach was the responsibility of the districts, and since the district structures had remained basically intact, the only uncertainty was whether the national church would be capable of assuming responsibility for pursuing mission opportunities beyond our own borders. There had been much discussion as to LCC's ability to undertake this new privilege, both by the Ways and Means Committee and by the All-Canada Church Workers' Conference of 1987. The reference in Acts 1:8—to "Jerusalem and in all Judea and Samaria, and to the ends of the earth"—was often cited as though it were a divinely ordered strategy for carrying out the Great Commission. But we soon discovered that these words gave the church (and, for that matter, every Christian) a mission mandate, but not necessarily a precise mission strategy. The latter needs to be flexible and depends more on God's opening of doors for the Gospel than it does on the church's desire to venture forth into a specific mission field.

As a young church, we began our overseas mission activity rather cautiously. We put our toes in the water, as it were, before we were ready to dive right in. Our partner churches around the world helped us out. We worked together with the Bleckmar Mission Society of Germany by supporting evangelistic and social ministry projects in Zaire (now known as the Democratic Republic of the Congo); with the Lutheran Church in France in the production of worship and educational resources for our French speaking pastors; and with the Lutheran church in Finland to translate the catechism into Russian, distributing 10,000 copies throughout the former Soviet Union with the help of the Lutheran Laymen's League. We even partnered with the Lutheran Church of Australia in funding theological education for pastors in Indonesia.

When the time came to venture into a foreign field on our own, we did not decide where to go. In each of the three foreign fields which presented themselves as mission opportunities, it was not because of our strategy but because of God's intervention. Each of them has its own story, and they are worth sharing.[6]

In the fall of 1989, I was to attend a meeting of the International Lutheran Conference in Seoul, South Korea. My wife and I had also made plans to incorporate into our travel plans a brief visit into China. However, in June of that year the Chinese government launched a bloody crackdown on pro-democracy demonstrators in Tiananmen Square in Beijing. Obviously, our desire to go to China at that time quickly evaporated.

With reservations already made, we looked for an alternative destination. Having long been fascinated with Thailand, but never having visited there, we decided that this would be our alternate destination. As we made our plans, we heard of a young Thai, named Ted Na Thalang, who was a student at Concordia Seminary, St. Louis. Currently on his vicarage in Minnesota, he not only gave us some valuable information regarding our travel plans, but suggested that we should go to southern Thailand and visit members of his family who lived in Takua Pa. His step-father, Herb Gernand, had served in the U.S. army, and while in south-east Asia, married Ted's mother, Staphorn. They relocated to North Dakota, with the expectation of spending the rest of their years there.

But God had other plans for them. He wanted them back in Thailand. As it turned out, Staphorn's father, who had been operating a large private school (nearly a thousand K-12 students) became critically ill and subsequently died. Staphorn felt obligated to return to Thailand to take over the school lest it be disbanded or taken over

---

6   Please accept the writer's apologies, but some stories can only be told in the first person.

by the government. Of course, Herb went as well, and soon, through the personal witnessing and encouragement of Herb and Staphorn, a small group of teachers, older students, and parents had become Christian. All this was in an area of Thailand that is less than two percent Christian. We enjoyed the opportunity to visit and worship with these new Christians, encouraging them in their faith and visiting some of the Christians in nearby villages.

A year and a half later when Ted graduated from the seminary and received his first call, it was, not surprisingly, as a missionary to Bangkok, Thailand, where the LCMS already had some educational and social ministry personnel. However, LCC contracted with him to make one or two visits a month to Takua Pa, to preach, administer the sacraments and, if possible, reach out to neighbouring towns and villages. That mission continues to this day with two congregations, both served by Thai pastors, and four preaching stations.

About sixty years earlier, in another part of the world, a God-fearing couple secretly brought their baby boy Mikhail, to their local Russian Orthodox priest to be baptized.[7] Little did the Gorbachev couple know that he would eventually become the most powerful man in the Soviet hierarchy. Elected as the General Secretary of the Communist Party in 1985, he totally changed the political system, the economic system, and even the daily life of the Russian people. By the end of 1991, the U.S.S.R. was no more. Daily life was still difficult, but there was now freedom of speech, of movement, and, to a fair extent, freedom of religion, not only in Russia itself, but in most of the former republics that made up the old U.S.S.R.

Not knowing how long the new freedoms would last, many

---

7   That Gorbachev was baptized is well documented. That it was done in secret is a reasonable assumption because of the religious persecution at the time.

sought to make contacts with western religious or relief organizations, with mixed motives. In response to some of the inquiries received in western Canada, several pastors, among them Karl Keller, Don Schiemann, and Bill Ney travelled to Ukraine, distributing Bibles and other religious materials, showing Christian films, and engaging ordinary people wherever there was opportunity. While it seemed clear that some listeners were primarily interested in how they could emigrate to Canada, others were genuinely interested in learning more about the Christian faith, having spent many years without the benefit of Christian congregations and pastors, most of which had been outlawed.

Around this time, LCC's Board for Mission Services decided it was time to call our first full-time Director of World Missions. After interviewing several candidates, the Board issued a call to Dr. Leonard Harms, who, at that time was on the World Missions staff of the LCMS, serving as area secretary for American Indian Missions. He previously had responsibility for American Asian Ministry, Jewish Ministry, and Eritrean ministry. Since he had proven capable of adapting to such a variety of cultures, our Board felt that Harms could also make whatever adjustments would be necessary for service in Canada. He accepted the call and was installed as Director of World Missions in February 1991.

With contacts already having been made in Ukraine, Harms led the next group of volunteers to examine more carefully what kind of opportunities for work in Ukraine there really were. He finally decided that the cities of Lviv and Dnepropetrovsk had contacts who were genuinely interested in hearing more about the Gospel and would also commit themselves to caring for whatever mission personnel we would send. Obviously they were not expected to cover all the financial costs, but they were asked to uphold and encourage the missionaries, take local responsibility for promoting the mission, and help the missionaries in the day-to-day situations they would face.

Rev. Dr. Leonard Harms, installed as LCC's Director of World Missions in February 1991.

After consulting with district office staff as to who would make good candidates to follow through on the opportunities Ukraine appeared to offer, Harms recommended to the Board for Mission Services that Rev. Roland Syens, then of Walnut Grove, B.C., and Rev. Keith Haberstock, of Whitecourt, Alberta, should be called. In December of 1992 Syens and Haberstock (with his wife Barbara) came to Winnipeg for orientation and basic language training, arriving in their respective mission destinations on January 25, 1993. In Lviv, the Haberstocks made contact with a group of Russian-speaking Germans who had no pastor but were led by several "elders." In addition there was a separate group of university students who were interested in learning more of the Christian faith. Bible studies and outreach efforts were undertaken with both groups. Meanwhile in Dnepropetrovsk, Syens' ministry centered on a large group of young

Ukraine Missionaries circa 1992: Rev. Roland Syens; Rev. Keith and Barb Haberstock; Irena Sharshakova, Translator; and LCC Director of World Missions, Rev. Dr. Leonard Harms.

families and university students. Since there was a Lutheran congregation in the city he sought to refer new converts to that congregation, although this met with limited success due to the primarily German ministry of that congregation. Syens' outreach, however, was very successful among others who had a thirst for the Gospel, including young people and prisoners.

In May of 1993, God opened a totally unexpected door that brought long term changes to the mission work in Ukraine. Following the collapse of the U.S.S.R., Lutherans from various parts of Russia "came out of the woodwork," as it were, and were augmented by Lutherans from Siberia and Kazakhstan, with the eventual goal of migrating to their ancestral homes in Germany (East and

West Germany had, by now, been reunited.) The Lutheran World Federation (LWF), based in Geneva, had taken the opportunity to reorganize these migrants into various regional churches, all under the oversight of the Evangelical Lutheran Church of Russia and Other States (ELKRAS). Regional bishops were given the task of recruiting pastors and establishing Lutheran congregations (almost exclusively German-speaking). One of these regional churches was the German Evangelical Lutheran Church of Ukraine (DELKU).

Since LCC had now placed missionary personnel in Ukraine, I felt it was important to meet with LWF staff, to explain what our intentions were concerning work in Lviv and Dnepropetrovsk, and that we were not in competition with the work of DELKU. The LWF felt that I should speak with the bishop of ELKRAS, whom I then phoned to see if we could meet somewhere. He suggested it would be more fruitful if I met with the bishop of DELKU, a pastor by the name of Viktor Gräfenstein, who, they said, was in Germany at the time. Gräfenstein said that if I could get a flight to Hamburg, he would be happy to meet with me at the airport before I returned to Canada. Although we had never met before,[8] we took this very brief opportunity to get acquainted and to share our faith as brothers in Christ, and how we understood what it means to bear the name "Lutheran." Of course, I also informed him of our missionaries in Lviv and Dnepropetrovsk, and encouraged him to contact them.

Although DELKU was an autonomous body, the Lutheran Church in Bavaria was underwriting the costs of the young church and paying the salaries of its pastors. This meant that DELKU remained beholden to the Bavarian church, and was heavily influenced

---

8   Rev. Gräfenstein was to recognize me because I would be wearing a blue cap with the letters "LC-C".

by its liberal theology. In the months that followed, Gräfenstein had opportunity to interact with LCC's missionaries in Ukraine, and with others from LCC who visited the missionaries. As a result, when mission executive Leonard Harms and I visited with Gräfenstein in late 1995, his mind was made up. He would resign as bishop of DELKU and invite like-minded pastors and congregations to join his cause. Of course, he had to leave the consequences of this decision in God's hands. While LCC did not promise Gräfenstein any financial support, we did agree to his request that we help train pastors. This request was gladly honored, and various faculty members, especially from Concordia Lutheran Seminary in Edmonton, along with parish pastors, worked under primitive conditions to help train a ministerium that could serve the emerging congregations of the new church. When dealing with biblical and theological issues, accurate translation is critical. The instructors were blessed with excellent local translators, as exemplified by Olga Koshaleva of Lviv.[9]

In one sense, this was an undertaking quite separate from what our missionaries in Ukraine were doing. At the same time, it is obvious that we would never have made contact with Gräfenstein, if we had not first sent those missionaries to Ukraine. Furthermore, it was helpful for Gräfenstein and his new congregations to know that they not only had support from a sister church far away in Canada, but that we had representatives right in their own country, whom they could consult as the need arose and whose presence demonstrated that LCC would continue to remain engaged in Ukraine. Rev. Gräfenstein has since retired, but all the other pastors of the church have been educated at the church's own Concordia Seminary,

---

9   Olga has since moved to Canada. Her married surname is Gudim.

located on the outskirts of Odessa. Two of the Ukrainian pastors also spent two years of advanced study in Canada: Oleg Schewtschenko at St. Catharines and Alexey Navrotskiy in Edmonton.[10] How LCC responded with providing theological education for the emerging church is described more completely in the account provided by Dr. Ralph Mayan.

It's worth asking, "Why would Gräfenstein find it so hard to accept mentoring from the Bavarian church?" Gräfenstein, and most of those who came with him, had made the journey from Kazakhstan. Like the rest of the U.S.S.R, it had been under the iron fist of atheistic communism, with Christian churches—other than a few Russian Orthodox congregations—virtually eliminated. When Christians are persecuted for their faith, one of two things will happen. Either they will deny their faith, as some unfortunately did, or they will treasure their faith even more. And as they treasure it, they become more resistant to anything that compromises what they have believed and for which they were willing to die. The Bavarian church, on the other hand, now forty years after the demise of the Third Reich, had become very wealthy and also very liberal in its theology. Those who followed Gräfenstein now had to decide whether they were willing to abandon their convictions for the sake of the financial benefits offered by the Bavarian church or abandon the Bavarian church for the sake of their convictions. For Gräfenstein, and for those congregations and pastors who followed him, the choice was clear.

The third mission field that LCC entered, in Nicaragua, will be described in the next major section of this work, since it began during the presidency of Dr. Ralph Mayan.

---

10   Navrotskiy also received a Master of Divinity degree from the Edmonton seminary.

Complementing the mission work which the synod was beginning to undertake, two auxiliary organizations which served the federation were restructuring to serve the new synod. The Lutheran Laymen's League of Canada continued its outreach ministry through Canadian radio stations, while also cooperating with LCC in equipping laity for Gospel outreach on the congregational level.

The Lutheran Women's Missionary League chose to establish itself as a sister organization to the International LWML. To that end, the Canadian members of the League invited their American sisters to participate in a joint convention in Edmonton in 1994. Eloise Schaan of Kanata, Ontario, was elected as the first president of the league, which celebrated its 25th anniversary in 2019.

Inter-Church Relations

With the adoption of the various documents that established the autonomous church, the founding convention also affirmed that LCC would continue to be in full altar and fellowship with the LCMS. That arrangement has continued to be a blessing to both churches and it is difficult even to imagine anything different. Pastors and other church workers are free to accept calls from one synod to the other, as are graduates from the respective terminal schools.

However, even though it was assumed that we would maintain the same relationship with other sister church bodies that we enjoyed as part of the LCMS, it also seemed appropriate in some cases to take specific actions to formalize that relationship. At its 1990 convention, the first one after being constituted, LCC formally declared altar and pulpit fellowship with the Evangelical Lutheran Church of England (ELCE) and the Independent Evangelical Lutheran Church of Germany (SELK). These churches were chosen because the former represents our political roots as part of the Commonwealth, and the latter our theological roots in the homeland of the Reformation. The chairman of the ELCE, Rev. Arnold Rakow and the bishop of SELK, Rev. Jobst Schoene, were both present at the convention to sign the relevant documents.

While interactions with the ELCE go back to the early days of World War II, when Rev. E. George Pierce, a Canadian, was sent by the LCMS to establish a congregation in London (and later to become the church's first chairman), both the LCMS and LCC have continued to provide pastors and theological instructors for the ELCE. The St. Catharines seminary has a particularly close relationship with Westfield House, which serves as the seminary of the ELCE. LCC has also enjoyed sharing pastors and guest instructors with SELK and has cooperated with SELK's Bleckmar Mission Society, particularly in Africa.

As the Lutheran Church-Hong Kong Synod (LCHKS) became more apprehensive about plans for returning the independent enclave to mainland China in 1997, there was a desire on the part of LCHKS pastors to seek calls in Canada, especially for work among the growing numbers of Hong Kong residents who were emigrating. Accordingly, provisions were made to facilitate the calling of such pastors, especially to the urban areas in the lower mainland of British Columbia and in the Greater Toronto area. At the request of Rev. Benjamin Chung, president of LCHKS, we also provided formal documentation which verified that Lutheran Church–Canada was a partner church with the LCHKS, in case there would be attempts by the Beijing government to isolate the LCHKS from relations with overseas churches.

In 1991, Dr. Lance Steicke, then president of the Lutheran Church of Australia (LCA), approached Lehman about the possibility of establishing fellowship with Lutheran Church–Canada. The early history of the LCA was very similar to that of the LCMS, with Lutherans opposed to the "Prussian Union" leaving Germany in search of a place that would allow them to practice their faith without governmental interference. Until 1965 there were two major Lutheran bodies in Australia, one of them in altar and pulpit fellowship with the American Lutheran Church, one more inclined to the LCMS (but not in formal fellowship). When they decided to merge, they did so on the condition that they would sever all formal relationships with other church bodies, with the exception of the Lutheran churches in Papua New Guinea where both churches had active mission fields. Since that merger, relationships with other Lutherans have always been on a case-by-case basis.

Steicke felt that sufficient time had passed, and with LCC being a new church, it was time to consider a more formal relationship. The first step was an exchange of faculty members between Concordia Lutheran Seminary in Edmonton and the LCA seminary in Adelaide. In December 1992, a delegation consisting of representatives from the Commission on Theology and Church Relations, the Council of Presidents, and the synod president met for three days with counterparts from the LCA. In the end, a document entitled "Recognition of Relationship: A Confessional Agreement" was drafted for presentation to the respective conventions of the two churches. The agreement provided for all the privileges we normally associate with altar and pulpit fellowship except for the fact that before a pastor could be considered for a call from one church to the other, prior approval had to be given by both the respective district and national presidents.

The LCA had no objection to us referring to this as an agreement for Altar and Pulpit Fellowship. It was just that because of their historic problems with the term, they preferred not to incorporate that term into the document's title. The fact that the document was, however, described as a confessional agreement underscored that the essential requirements for altar and pulpit fellowship, that is, agreement in doctrine and practice, did exist between the churches. Dr. Steicke was a guest at our 1993 convention, at which he and Lehman signed the formal documents.

Although our two churches have much in common, the sheer distance that separates us meant that there would not be as much interaction as, for example, with the LCMS. However, a significant number of pastoral exchanges have taken place, along with visiting instructors at seminaries. Presidents continue to attend conventions of each other's church. The ABC District of LCC even established a special partnership with the New South Wales district of the LCA.

In the fall of 1993, at a meeting of the International Lutheran Council, the Rev. Leopoldo Heimann, president of the Evangelical Lutheran Church of Brazil (IELB) suggested to Lehman that our two churches consider the possibility of a formal relationship of Altar and Pulpit Fellowship. Our CTCR agreed that this would be desirable, and in January 1994, President Heimann met with representatives of our CTCR, Council of Presidents, and President Lehman to discuss our respective commitments to biblical and Confessional Lutheranism. In June of that year, when IELB was observing its 90th anniversary, delegates recommended establishing altar and pulpit fellowship with Lutheran Church–Canada. Lehman was invited to be a guest at their convention. Lehman, in turn, asked LCC's treasurer, Ken Werschler, to accompany him. Werschler also presented the Brazilian church with lapel pins depicting the logo of the IELB.[11]

Heimann was a guest at LCC's 1996 convention in Edmonton, where we passed the resolution declaring our two churches to be in church fellowship, after which the formal agreements were signed. One concrete outcome of this fellowship declaration is evident in the number of pastors who have accepted calls to serve in Canada. No fewer than eight pastors from the IELB have accepted calls to Canada. The first to do so was Rev. Gilvan de Azevedo, of Brasilia, who accepted a call to First Lutheran Church in Windsor, Ontario.

International Lutheran Council

The International Lutheran Council (ILC) is a global association of some 54 Lutheran Churches that had its origins in the aftermath of World War II, when Lutheran Churches in Europe were in need of gathering members who had been scattered during the war, restoring church buildings and resuming their programs of theological education. The first meeting was held in Uelzen, Germany at the invitation of the LCMS, followed two years later by a similar meeting in Oakland, California. Initially, it identified itself as International Lutheran Theological Conference, and then simply as International Lutheran Conference. In 1993, it adopted a more formal constitution after which it identified itself as the International Lutheran Council.

Although representatives from Canada, among them Dr.

---

11   The parents of both Ken Werschler and of his wife, Dorothy, served as LCMS missionaries in Brazil, when that church was still a district of the LCMS.

Schwermann, Elroy Treit, and Roy Holm attended some of the meetings prior to autonomy, LCC was now welcomed as a full member of the ILC. Since, by virtue of its size, LCMS was perceived by some as overpowering the council, many of the smaller churches saw LCC as being small enough to identify with them, yet strong enough to provide support and leadership. As a result, both Lehman and Mayan served extended terms as chairmen, and President Bugbee served as vice-chairman. After retiring as president of LCC, Bugbee continues to serve on the ILC executive committee. In addition, faculty members of LCC seminaries made important contributions to the International Seminaries Conferences, sponsored by the ILC.

From 1993-1998, Lehman also served as editor of ILC News, the Council's quarterly publication. LCC's Mathew Block, editor of *The Canadian Lutheran*, continues to serve as communications manager for the ILC.

Communications

From its earliest days, The Lutheran Church—Missouri Synod published regular periodicals for the general edification of both pastors and laity. In 1871, Adam Ernst was instrumental in publishing *Das Lutherisches Volksblatt* for Ontario readers. Around 1936, Canada's two western districts launched a regional publication called *The Canadian Lutheran*. In

Ian Adnams, LCC
Communications Director

more recent times, *The Lutheran Witness*, published by the LCMS, included district supplements to replace any free-standing district publications. However, the Board of Directors of the LCC Federation determined that a national newsmagazine was necessary, and in June 1986 appointed Fran Wershler of Winnipeg as editor of *The Canadian Lutheran*, serving all of Canada. The separate regional publications were discontinued. After the constituting convention, Werschler produced a special "newspaper format" edition with extensive coverage of the convention.

With the impact that computers were having on the "information age," it became apparent to LCC's Board for Communication Services (BCS), that it was time to engage a full-time Director of Communications, who would not only serve as editor of *The Canadian Lutheran*, but also help LCC embrace the new technologies that were transforming both routine office work and the proclamation of the Gospel.

As the BCS began its search for the newly created position, Bob Hallman of Kitchener, Ontario briefly succeeded Fran Wershler as editor of *The Canadian Lutheran*, from January 1993 to December 1994. At that time, Ian Adnams, who, had been employed by Concordia College in Edmonton accepted the invitation to serve as Director of Communications for LCC. *The Canadian Lutheran* became more of a magazine than a newspaper, offering submissions by various writers regarding theological and ethical issues, and with more extended coverage from LCC's mission fields and post-secondary institutions. In addition, a lay-oriented theological periodical, *Word and Deed*, was issued quarterly, addressing current doctrinal and moral issues. Eventually, with the inclusion of more theological and doctrinal articles in *The Canadian Lutheran*, the publication of *Word and Deed* was discontinued.

During Adnams' tenure, *The Canadian Lutheran*, its editor, and various writers won numerous awards from the Canadian Church Press, both for individual articles and for specific writers.

After Bill Buller's retirement in 1995, Adnams also served as convention manager for the synod's triennial conventions.

Another Form of Ministry—the Diaconate

At the time of LCC's autonomy, the LCMS already had established programs at its various universities for the training of church workers who were not pastors. Some of these were specifically designated as deaconesses, others as teachers, parish workers, directors of education, directors of evangelism, and so forth. Some of these also served in Canada. To clarify their status on the synodical roster, the LCMS had established two broad categories: Minister of Religion – Ordained (which included all clergy members), and Minister of Religion – Commissioned (which included all non-clergy members.) Educational requirements varied for commissioned ministers, as did the institution providing the training.

Even before LCC became autonomous, it was obvious that we could not duplicate the LCMS model, but we did need parochial school teachers. As for the other categories, Concordia College (now Concordia University) had, under the presidency of Dr. Orville Walz, called Jeannette Lietzau to its faculty and assigned her the task of developing a program for training "Directors of Parish Services." These individuals would develop specialties in such areas as evangelism, youth or seniors ministry, Christian education, and so forth.

In an attempt to recognize the diversity of gifts and the important contributions which appropriately trained lay members, both male and female, could make for the health of congregations and the general welfare of LCC, the 1996 convention had before it a recommendation to establish the office of "deacon" to include all church worker offices other than clergy. Thus there would be a "ministerial roster" and a "diaconal roster." Members on either roster would be "members of the synod," with certain rights and privileges held in common, but in some cases diverging.

Although extensive background documentation was presented on the matter, the 1996 convention felt that opportunity should be given for discussion at the local and circuit levels before proceeding with implementation. As a result, final approval was not given until the 1999 convention.

As of January 2021, there were 25 deacons on the active roster. Of these, ten were parochial school teachers eligible for service in settings ranging from pre-school to high school. The second largest group consisted of those who served as "Directors of Parish Services." Twenty-six are currently not serving, but hold candidate status, and eleven are retired.

Postlude

The 1996 convention held in Edmonton—the last one I would chair—provided an opportunity to reflect on all the initiatives that the new church had undertaken in the previous eight years. God had been good to us—far better than we deserved. The journey undertaken by Dr. A.H. Schwermann and those who travelled with him had been long and winding, with numerous detours along the way. But the transforming leap of faith that finally gave birth to an autonomous Lutheran Church in Canada had been safely taken. Metaphorically speaking, one could say that we had crossed the Jordan. And it was all in God's time and according to His plan. God had blessed us with a strong sense of unity. He had opened doors of opportunity, bringing the Gospel to lands we would not have entered had we not been autonomous. We were training our own pastors and lay leaders, with two excellent seminaries[12] and a college that was on the verge of becoming a fully accredited university.

Not surprisingly, some of our good intentions did not materialize. We did not manage to deal with our cumbersome structure as we said we would. We did not challenge our people to be more supportive with the financial blessings God had given them. We did not successfully pursue the resolutions asking us to find alternate methods of funding our mission. The journey ahead of us would be harder than the one we had traveled thus far.

But a new day was dawning. A new president would be elected, bringing new gifts and new energies to the task. A new mission field in Nicaragua would blossom, and a mission society would create new support for sharing the Gospel. A fully functioning diaconate would provide new opportunities for service in God's kingdom, as would a program for preparing pastors with alternate training. God had used us as His instrument, and there would be much more to come. We said it at our founding convention. There was even greater reason to say it again: *"Soli Deo Gloria!"*

---

12   In particular, the seminaries provided us with sufficient faculty expertise to undertake the training of indigenous pastors in each of LCC's mission fields.

LCC Youth Gathering in Thunder Bay 1989.

LCC Youth Gathering in Saskatoon 1992.

1996-2008

LUTHERAN CHURCH–CANADA

Ralph Mayan

I leave the writing of a formal history of my years of service to a future researcher and historian. My assignment is to contribute to a history of the formation of Lutheran Church–Canada by preparing a recollection of significant events during the time of my service. (By God's grace, all three presidents who have served LCC since its formation are still living and have consented to this enterprise.) My years of service began in September 1996 and continued through to September 2008. I also had the privilege of serving as Temporary Mission Executive for approximately one more year while the Synod in consultation with the newly elected president prepared to call a new person to this position.

In preparation for writing this chapter, I consulted with the two administrative officers who served Lutheran Church–Canada during my years of service: Dr. Leonard Harms, the International Mission

Executive (1991-2006) and Dr. Ian Adnams, Director of Communications (1995-2010). I wish to express my thanks to both as they were most helpful in identifying significant events that had a positive impact upon the Synod.

"Where there is no vision. . . ."

It was not an hour after my election that someone came to me and asked, "What is your vision for the Synod?" I have to admit that at the time I was not thinking about vision, but the question led me to reflect on this verse from Proverbs[1] and the awesome responsibility that God was placing upon me—one that could not be accomplished but by His grace and mercy. Over the weeks and months that followed that convention, the question remained front and centre. In fact, it made me a little nervous. Visions are what God gave to His prophets of old. I'm not a prophet in that sense and have not received any such vision from God. I do however have dreams.

What is my dream for Lutheran Church–Canada? In a sense that question is easy to answer. I would like to see it grow to be twice or even three-times its size. I would like to see our churches filled for worship, our Bible classes overflowing. I would like to see our Synod have so much money that we could do every mission project and take up every mission opportunity that comes our way. And the list of dreams could go on and on.

But having said all this, and recognizing that it is good to have dreams, there is one problem: they centre on results and as such are not under our control. Whether people come to faith or grow in their faith, whether they grow in their love for the Lord and their service to Him, that is the work of the Holy Spirit. It depends upon the grace

---

1   29:18.

of God. Now I know that this kind of language is sometimes used as an excuse for inactivity. That is not my intention. I mention it because I believe it is important to recognize who we are and what our task is. We are instruments; we are tools used by God. We are part of the process with the result being in the hands of God.[2] Thus, in seeking to define that vision, I sought to see it in terms of process, asking the question, "How can the Synod and I personally assist its members, the pastors, deacons, and congregations of Synod, to carry out the task that Christ has given to His church, the task of 'making disciples'?" The vision developed included the following three principles:

Principle One: Strengthening our Synod's biblical and confessional foundations. My vision was to encourage and strengthen our seminaries and college in the work they do on behalf of Synod preparing pastors and deacons for the church. One cannot stress the importance of this too much. Pastors, their theology, their ability to communicate and teach, to sacrifice and to serve all have a marked influence on the future of the church. This is not to deny the work of the Holy Spirit, but to affirm the high standard that God sets for pastors and deacons in their calling. It also meant sensitising those labourers to engage in a "continuing education" program so that they might continue to grow through a disciplined course of study. It meant encouraging and strengthening our pastoral conferences and circuit meetings as opportunities for study and prayer. It was also my goal to encourage our pastors to lead the men and women in their congregations into the Word so that they too might grow in faith and service because it is only through the Word that the Spirit

---

2   St. Paul reminds us of this in 1 Corinthians 3:5-9.

creates, sustains, and strengthens faith.[3]

Principle Two: Strengthening our Synod's vision for Mission. Mission is what the church is all about. It was important that the church understand that the mission of the church was changing as we approached the twenty-first century. Our world and our country had changed. We were now living in the midst of the mission field, and every encounter we had might be an opportunity God is giving "to share the hope that is within us." We also needed to counter the Canadian mentality that speaks of sharing the faith as not "caring." After speaking with both lay and clergy it also became clear that we had to do a better job of telling the story of what God was doing in mission through His church.

Principle Three: Strengthening the care we give to one another in the church and in the communities in which we live. No one would dispute that we live in a hurting world and that Christ calls us to respond. It is a call to love and care for one another, both in the church and in the community. Indeed, such "caring" is an integral part of being in mission. There was also a need to evaluate our international social ministry mission and develop a better working relationship with Canadian Lutheran World Relief.

Throughout the twelve years of service, these three principles served as an overriding guide to carrying out the individual responsibilities assigned in my service as president. It was interesting to hear Dr. Adnams state that these principles also served as a guide for

---

3   Under this principle I include also the important work carried out through the International Lutheran Council, a worldwide association of confessional Lutheran Churches, in encouraging and strengthening each other in our biblical and confessional foundations. In addition to gatherings of the heads of churches, the ILC hosted gatherings of theological educators from these confessional churches in order that they might support and encourage each other in their task. All three presidents of LCC served in leadership positions in this organization.

LCC Council of Presidents 1988. Back: Revs. Albin Stanfel, Karl Koslowsky, Roy Holm, Harold Ruf; Front: Orval Walz, Edwin Lehman, Robert Bugbee.

him as he carried out his responsibilities in communications. Insofar as we were guided by these principles and experienced the blessings of the Spirit, we give thanks to God. Where we failed in the task to which we were called, we ask God's forgiveness and the forgiveness of the church.

***

"Now to Him who is able to do far more abundantly than all that we ask or think, according to the power at work within us, to Him be glory in the church and in Christ Jesus throughout all generations, forever and ever." - Ephesians 3:20-21

Far more abundantly than all that we ask or think... in International Mission.

God richly blessed His mission carried out through Lutheran Church–Canada. One such blessing —a significant development

*LCC Council of Presidents 2000. Back: Revs. Ralph Mayan,
Dan Rinderknecht, Roy Holm, Roger Winger. Front: Revs. James Fritsche,
Harold Ruf, Dennis Putzman.*

in the mission of the church—was the establishment of theological education as the primary vehicle for international mission. While the shift enabled the church to multiply labourers for the kingdom and proved to be cost-effective, and while the shift happened differently in the three areas of mission, Dr. Harms describes this shift as the natural outcome of following St. Paul's mission strategy as recorded in the book of Acts. In each of his mission journeys, St. Paul would travel from community to community sharing the Gospel of Jesus Christ trusting that the Holy Spirit would work faith and bring together a community of believers. He would then, together with the community, identify labourers for the Kingdom according to the criteria described in his letters (1 Timothy 3; Titus 1). These individuals would be prepared for ministry (2 Timothy 2) and following preparation serve as pastors, deacons, and deaconesses in their respective congregations (Acts 20:17ff). The missionary's task in those communities would then be completed and the missionary would move to a new field of mission.

Our mission in Ukraine began in 1993. Rev. Keith Haberstock and his wife Barbara were sent to Lviv, Ukraine. Rev. Roland Syens was assigned to Dnepropetrosk. It was during their outreach in these communities, primarily with university students, that they also became acquainted with Rev. Victor Gräfenstein and a small confessional church in Ukraine under his leadership. He had previously met with Dr. Lehman in an airport in Hamburg, Germany and there was an instant recognition that they shared a common understanding of what it meant to be a confessional Lutheran. He was a troubled leader in the liberal German Evangelical Lutheran Church in Ukraine (DELKU) and was under increasing pressure to follow their more liberal theology. Indeed, a special synod had been called in which he was to defend his more conservative theological position. He requested assistance from LCC, asking whether we might send someone to present a paper on confessional Lutheranism. Dr. Threinen consented to do so. Later, Rev. Gräfenstein would describe Threinen's paper as the best presentation made at the conference. Indeed, it also clarified some things in his own mind.

Dr. Lehman would meet again with Rev. Gräfenstein along with Dr. Harms in November 1995. At that time, he and several other congregations announced that they were leaving DELKU and were going to establish what is today called the Synod of Evangelical Lutheran Churches in Ukraine (SELKU). Most of the members of these congregations were of German heritage, returning to Ukraine from Siberia where they had been exiled during Stalin's regime. They felt very much alone with only one ordained pastor assisted by "brothers" who would lead worship in their respective congregations. Rev. Gräfenstein and these brothers found a kindred spirit in their association with missionaries Syens and Haberstock. Both Dr. Lehman and Dr. Harms encouraged this association.

I had the privilege of meeting with Rev. Gräfenstein and the brothers of this church in August 1997. Seeking to affirm our unity in confession, we gathered around a brief study of the Augsburg Confession. It was during this study that a most interesting event took place: Rev. Syens arrived with a newly completed translation of the Book of Concord. Our discussion was set aside as these brothers took the opportunity to explore the book and read to one another sections from it. What a joy it was to witness their joy in receiving this new resource. Following that meeting, Dr. Harms and I made a commitment on behalf of LCC to further our relationship by providing theological education for the brothers of the church. This meeting was followed by a weeklong intensive course led by Dr. Edward Kettner, a member of the faculty of Concordia Lutheran Seminary in Edmonton.

In due course, the Board for Missions and Social Ministry requested Concordia Lutheran Seminary to oversee a program of seminary education for the SELCU, and Dr. Norman Threinen was called to serve as the first rector of that program. Funding was provided through Concordia Lutheran Mission Society from the Marvin M. Schwann Foundation.[4] The first class of seven graduated in July 2001. One of those graduates would be assigned to Dnepepetrosk as pastor and missionary. This program of theological education in Ukraine continues to this very day.

---

4   CLMS would also be involved in supporting the building of the seminary in years to come.

Our missionaries returned to Canada after approximately ten years of service: Rev. Haberstock in 1998 and Rev. Syens in 2005. Their task was completed. We now pray God's blessing upon this small confessional Lutheran Church in Ukraine and their theological education program as they take ownership of Gospel proclamation in their own country.

***

The development and transition to theological education as the primary vehicle for mission in Thailand was very different from that in Ukraine. No missionaries were ever sent from Lutheran Church–Canada. While The Lutheran Church—Missouri Synod had done some initial work in the Takuapa area of South Thailand, the community of believers established in the area came about through the witness of Dr. Herbert Gernand, a retired engineer from North Dakota and his wife Staphorn. Believing they were called to witness to their faith, they shared the Gospel with coworkers in the school operated by Staphorn Gernand and with their neighbours. When a community of faith developed, they began the initial process of identifying labourers for ministry. These included Suchart Srikakahn and Suchat Chijit who were identified to serve as pastoral candidates along with their wives who were already serving as evangelists.

Because Dr. Gernand had completed some theological study at Concordia Seminary in St. Louis, Missouri, he was equipped to provide some basic theological education to these students. He used some materials already translated into Thai, but was also assisted by his wife who translated other materials that he thought would be helpful in teaching basic biblical knowledge. One such set of books was Concordia's Teacher Training materials used for preparing Sunday

School Teachers in North America. He also prepared sermons and had them translated into Thai so that these men would be able to lead in worship. Dr. Gernand held strongly to the premise that sharing and teaching the faith should be carried out in the language of the people. He rejected English as a second language as a tool for outreach.

Dr. Lehman was the first to visit the Gernands in 1991. Their visit was one of those encounters that could only be arranged by God. Dr. Lehman and his wife had planned to travel to China on vacation. However, as a result of the political instability resulting from the demonstrations in Tiananmen Square, their plans had to change. At the encouragement of Rev. Victor Fry and Vicar Ted Nathalong—a Thai student at Concordia Seminary in St. Louis and stepson of Herb Gernand, serving his year of vicarage in Minnesota— they decided to travel to Thailand instead, visiting one of the resorts near Phuket. While there, they visited with Herb and Staphorn Gernand and learned firsthand about their mission. While no request was made for any assistance at the time, it was certainly felt that something more might develop in the future. When Ted Nathalong graduated from the seminary, he received a call from LCMS World Missions to serve in Bangkok, Thailand. LCC saw this as an opportunity to assist the Gernands in their mission and contracted with him to visit Takuapa twice a month to lead worship.

Our relationship grew with this small community of believers through the visits of Dr. Harms, LCC's Mission Executive. It ultimately led to a commitment to develop a pastoral education program that would follow the sixteen courses of basic biblical study led by Dr. Gernand. The pastoral education program closely followed the outline of courses used in our seminaries, with additional input from the local church.

Arrangements were also made to free Staphorn Gernand from her teaching duties so that she could serve as a translator. Two young women from Canada, Senga Boesche and Amy Fritsche, volunteered to serve as ESL teachers in Thailand for one year. Others would follow in subsequent years. Intensive two-week classes began in 1998 with pastors from LCC serving as instructors. Among them were Revs. Mark Beiderweiden, William Ney, Albert Schmidt, Colin Liske, Missionary Sandor Arguello from Nicaragua, and Dr. William Mundt from Concordia Lutheran Theological Seminary in St. Catharines, Ontario. The first Thai pastor, Rev. Suchat Chijit, was ordained in January 2002. I was privileged to participate in that ordination. The second, Rev. Suchart Srikakahn, was ordained in 2003. Rev. Chijit continues to serve as a full-time pastor and missionary throughout the Panga Province. Rev. Srikakahn serves as a worker-priest.

Since this initial program of theological education, additional programs have been operated by the Luther Institute Southeast Asia (LISA), an organization whose leadership includes members from LCMS, LCC, Sahatay Lutheran Church, and Lutherans from the Bangkok area. This organization, with the support of LCC, has expanded its work into Cambodia, preparing Cambodian pastors and deaconesses to serve the church and reach out to those who do not yet believe. Providing leadership to this organization and representing Lutheran Church–Canada is Dr. Leonard Harms.

Lutheran Church–Canada entered into a more formal relationship with Sahatay Lutheran Church, a church representing six communities of faith in the Panga Province in January 2002 following the ordination of their first pastor.

***

To understand the movement from missionary to theological education as the primary vehicle for Mission in Nicaragua, one needs to briefly review the history of this mission.

Following an exploratory visit to Nicaragua in 1995 and an invitation to begin mission work in Nicaragua, Lutheran Church–Canada called Nicaragua-born Rev. Sandor Arguello to serve as missionary. After some preparatory work in Winnipeg in 1997, he and his family moved back to Nicaragua, taking up residence in Chinandega. Initial work was difficult. Some of those who at first were positive about the mission had moved on; others seemed to have lost interest. God, however, had different plans.

In 1998, Hurricane Mitch hit, and the results were devastating in the Chinandega region. Hundreds died, homes were destroyed, and a food-shortage developed. God used this disaster to create an opportunity for care and witness, and at the centre of this activity was Rev. Arguello. With the support of various agencies of the church and a variety of Non-Governmental Organizations from around the world, he was able to provide emergency care in those hurting communities. Emergency shelters were provided, food was brought in, and even medical care was arranged. People soon learned that Rev. Arguello cared about them and could be trusted and—and so they gave him a listening ear.

Having developed administrative skills as a regional school superintendent in Nicaragua before the revolution, Rev. Arguello put those skills to work in providing care and witness. In each of the communities in which there was need, he had the communities elect one man and one woman to serve as care providers. They would

FROM AUTONOMY ONWARD | 165

come into Chinandega to receive their allotment of emergency rations. Rev. Arguello would instruct them in a Bible lesson and send them back into their communities to care and to witness. Each week they would come and each week he would send them back—and, by the power of the Spirit, communities of faith developed in Santa Patricia, Rancheria, La Joya, Potosi, El Realejo, Somotillo, El Bonete, Israel, Villa Salvadorita, El Viejo, and other places.

There was, however, only one missionary-pastor on the ground. How would these communities of faith grow to have Word and Sacrament ministry in their midst? Following the pattern of theological education now established in Ukraine and Thailand, and with the support of the Schwan Foundation, the LCC Board for Missions and Social Ministry in cooperation with Concordia Lutheran Theological Seminary in St. Catharines established a theological program to prepare pastors and deaconesses for the church. Students were identified in each of the communities by Rev. Arguello and the worshipping community. Many, though not all, were the original care providers identified at the very beginning.

The first theological education classes began in the Fall of 1999. The classes were taught as intensive two-week courses four times a year, held in several different retreat centres in the country. In later years the classes were held at the Mission Centre built and dedicated in 2006. Instructors were selected by Dr. Roger Humann from CLTS. During the time when the pastoral candidates were not in class, they would serve in their respective communities as vicars under the supervision of Rev. Arguello. The deaconess students also had their internships, working primarily with women and children.

The first class was completed in 2002 with thirteen pastors being ordained and sixteen deaconesses consecrated. Most of the newly ordained pastors were assigned to their respective communities of faith; several, however, were selected and sent out as missionaries to serve in communities not yet having a Gospel witness. My first visit to this mission field took place at this graduation and I was privileged to ordain and consecrate this class of students.

The second class began in 2004 and was completed in 2006, with seven pastors ordained and thirteen deaconesses consecrated for service. Again, most were sent back into the communities of faith from which they came. What was unusual about this class was that there were three additional Nicaraguan men who were serving as missionaries in Northern Nicaragua for individual Evangelical Lutheran Church of America (ELCA) congregations. Though aware of the confessional theological education that these candidates would receive in our program, they not only encouraged their attendance, but supported the costs of sending them.

Two additional theological education classes have since been held. A third program was completed in 2009 with three pastors ordained and nine deaconesses consecrated. A fourth class was completed in 2015 with eleven pastors ordained and nine deaconesses consecrated.

The church in Nicaragua, aware that theological education is never complete, further established a program of at least two one-week intensive programs of theological education each year, as well as a gathering of pastors and deaconesses for worship, study, and prayer twice a month. This program continues to this very day.

Following the graduation of the first class, it became apparent that the newly formed congregations and missions together with their pastors and deaconesses wanted to take more and more responsibility for the mission and ministry in their communities and country. The child was becoming a young adult. In 2006, a committee of pastors, deaconesses and lay members of the mission, with the encouragement of Lutheran Church–Canada, began to lay the foundations for the establishment of a Nicaraguan church body and prepare a constitution for this church. This work was completed in the winter of 2007 and a founding convention of the Lutheran Church Synod of Nicaragua (*Igelsia Luterana Sínodo de Nicaragua*) was held in January 2008.

In LCC's convention later that year, we recognized this new church as our partner in mission, establishing an altar and pulpit relationship with them. Rev. Sandor Arguello's work was now completed, and he resigned from this position in December 2008. It was my privilege following my retirement to spend significant amounts of time in Nicaragua working with the leadership of this new church and encouraging and supporting the pastors and deaconesses in their service.

***

Far more abundantly than all that we ask or think... in Canadian Mission.

The transition which established theological education as the primary vehicle for mission in the three areas of LCC mission led to the development of several other programs that have been significant in LCC and enabled LCC to expand her mission in Canada.

One such program was the "Pastors with Alternate Training" (PAT) program, adopted at the 2002 national convention. Two developments within Canada led to consideration of such a program. The first was the demographic shift taking place in the country and in the church. In the early days of our history, we were regarded as a rural church. Our thriving congregations were rural, and they supported much of the mission and ministry of the Synod. As the country urbanized, these rural congregations became smaller and smaller. More and more families were leaving the farm. Farms were getting larger, but the number of people needed to operate them was getting smaller, and that affected the size of our rural congregations. Many congregations began to struggle to maintain their own congregational mission and ministry. Some were on the verge of dismissing their pastor and closing their doors. The Council of Presidents added another column to their congregational statistics entitled "Vacant but not calling."

As this phenomenon developed, the Council of Presidents explored options for continuing Word and Sacrament ministry in these communities. They ranged from forming a "federation of two or more congregations" to the actual amalgamation of congregations. A question however remained. How could one carry on a regular Word and Sacrament ministry in those congregations distant from a neighbouring congregation?

In addition to this demographic shift taking place was the significant increase in refugees and immigrants coming from third world countries. This was a phenomenon that had led Dr. Edward Westcott, a former executive director of the LCMS Board for missions, to exclaim at an LCC federation convention back in the 1980s that the mission field was coming to North America and to Canada. An interesting pattern in this immigration was that some immigrants came as whole communities of people. Where that was not the case, they often sought out their cultural communities upon arrival in this new land. In this way they could share not only language and culture but in some cases their faith as well.

It was my privilege to meet such a community in Winnipeg: the Oromo community from Ethiopia. They gathered at several different LCC congregations in Winnipeg. Men were appointed by the community to serve as worship leaders very much like the "brothers" in Ukraine. Like them, these men also lacked adequate theological training. Their request for assistance was a kind of Macedonian call for help.

In a resolution passed at the 1999 Synod convention, the church acknowledged the challenges identified by the Council of Presidents and holding to the Augsburg Confession Article 14 that no one "should publicly teach or preach or administer the sacrament without a regular call," resolved that the Board of High Education convene a task force to explore an alternative way of preparing men for ordination into Word and Sacrament ministry, reporting back to the 2002 convention. The task force was to include representatives from the Council of Presidents, the Board for Higher Education, the Commission on Theology and Church Relations, the Seminaries, and the Board for Missions and Social Ministry Services.

The task force led by Dr. Paul Dorn began its task by requesting Dr. John Stevenson, a faculty member from Concordia Lutheran Theological Seminary as well as member of the CTCR, to draft a paper exploring the "Scriptural, Confessional and Constitutional Perspectives on the Establishment of a 'Special Needs Ministry' of Word and Sacrament." In addition to this document, the task force was able to study a document prepared by the Lutheran Church of Australia entitled "Pastoral Care of Isolated Members of the Lutheran Church of Australia." This document outlined a special needs program of theological education adopted by that church to provide Word and Sacrament ministry to the Aboriginal peoples of Australia.

In 2002, after thorough debate, the resolution "To Provide for the Certification, Ordination, and Installation of Pastors with Alternate Training" was adopted. The resolution proposed that LCC district presidents identify pastoral needs arising in situations similar to those noted above. The procedure for identifying potential candidates for the program would begin within the local community, in consultation with the district president and mission executive. The men identified must have served in leadership positions within their own congregation and have the respect of the community in which they reside. The Council of Presidents would then, in consultation with the seminaries of the Synod, supervise the preparation, training, and certification of "pastors with alternate training." The resolution also noted that PAT candidates would not "ordinarily" be available for calls to other parishes within the Synod.

Since the adoption of the program, there have been six graduates. Five of these graduates reflect outreach to ethnic communities: Rev. Asefa Aredo to the Oromo community; Rev. James Kay to the Sudanese community; Rev. Oboya Ochalla to the Anyuak community; Rev. Eduardo Rodriques to the Hispanic community; and Rev. Joseph Singh to the Punjabi community. There has also been one graduate for a geographically remote community: the congregation in High Prairie, in Northern Alberta. In 2017, Rev. Terry Goerz was certified and ordained into the Office of the Public Ministry. Rev. Goerz was the ideal candidate as envisioned by the Council of Presidents, having served for many years as a leader in his congregation in almost every area of service. He had also served on various boards at both the district and synodical level as well as with a variety of its auxiliaries.

At the time of writing, there are an additional six men preparing for certification and ordination. All come from ethnic communities across the country. God has certainly used this program to reach out to the ethnic communities in our nation.

Another program which grew out of our mission experience relates to the process of identifying future pastors and deacons for service in Lutheran Church–Canada. In all three areas of LCC mission, the identifying of candidates for ministry began in the local communities of faith. It was our desire to encourage such a practice within the Synod. The program was given the name "RSVP Church Worker Recruitment" and was initiated in January 1998.

The program was based on one being used in a diocese of the Roman Catholic Church in the Winnipeg area entitled "Called by Name." We adapted it for our use. Our approach centred upon the belief that God grows future pastors and deacons within the local congregation and those most likely to recognize them are the individuals who sit beside them in worship or teach them in Sunday School or Confirmation class. In a sense, this was already happening as pastors and Sunday School teachers encouraged students to think about preparing for service in the church. Our goal was to formalize the process and give the entire congregation a role in identifying those whom God might be calling to serve in ministry.

After discussions with our seminaries and college, a date was established for a Synod-wide recruitment Sunday at the end of

January. Materials were prepared for the weeks preceding the event to acquaint congregational members with the program and process. Special orders for worship were prepared for the Sunday together with inserts, sermon suggestions, and follow-up instructions.[5]

On the appointed Sunday, members were asked at the conclusion of the sermon to place on a provided recruitment form the names of individuals within their congregations whom they believed God might be calling to full-time service within the church. The local pastor was asked to visit with these individuals (together with their parents if they were children), and then forward the names to the Synod office. The president would write a personal letter of encouragement to the individual and forward the name to one of our seminaries or the college or in some cases, both. They in turn would place the name on their recruitment list and contact the individual either by letter or personal visit, sharing information about their institution.

As noted, the program began in 1998 and continued through 2006. Close to 500 young men and women were identified. Again, God blessed this program in that a number of pastors and deacons serving in LCC congregations were initially identified through the program. Only God knows how many identified are now serving as leaders and volunteers in their congregations because someone pointed out to them that God might be calling them to service. The RSVP program also caught the interest of The Lutheran Church—Missouri Synod who asked permission to use the program in their Synod for recruitment.

***

---

5   At the time of writing these materials are still available on the LCC website.

Far more abundantly than all that we ask or think... in Communications.

LCC Communications is another area where significant changes took place between the years 1996 and 2008. Upon arrival in the Synod office in the fall of 1996, the office was using an in-house Linux computer system for the drafting of documents and storing data but had no internet or email access. Email access at the time was only available through Ian Adnams, our communications executive, who brought his personal computer into the office and allowed us to use it. At the conclusion of my term, the office was well equipped with a Windows-based computer system, a well-designed webpage, internet, and email access, together with other communication tools that enabled the office to communicate with deployed staff as well as with our missionaries and foreign mission offices. What a blessing it was during my three month stay in Nicaragua after retirement to be able to communicate face to face with LCC office staff and mission committees.

These changes came about because of the work of the Board for Communication Services and its director, Ian Adnams, and the good working relationship established with LLL-Canada and its director, Steven Klinck. This Board had established as its overriding mission the goal of communicating the mission and ministry of LCC based on the vision established by the Board of Directors and the president. They used our internal media—*The Canadian Lutheran*, the webpage, email, LCC events—to help foster this identity as a national church. They also saw as their task the need to equip church workers and congregational leaders with their own communication skills so they could better reach out in their own communities. There was also the desire to provide training in the use of computers and other media for outreach. Finally, the Board sought to establish LCC as a reliable source of information and comment for national news organizations. It was in my first year that Ian Adnams and I travelled to Toronto to introduce ourselves to the religion editors of both *The National Post* and *The Globe and Mail* with a side visit to Vision TV. At that time, Vision TV was broadcasting the Lutheran Hour Ministry television program, "On Main Street."

In 1997, LCC launched its first website www.lutheranchurch-canada.ca. At that time regulations would not allow more generic addresses. When the regulations were relaxed, the domain name was changed to www.lutheranchurch.ca. The goal in using a more generic address was to establish LCC as the first Lutheran presence to appear on the website when a search was made using the word, Lutheran. Other LCC-related organizations followed suit: Lutheranwomen.ca, Lutheranyouth.ca, and Lutheranfoundation.ca.

It was in 1998 that the Board for Communication Services began the task of equipping congregations in the art of communication. Parish Media Teams training was a joint project of the Board for Communication Services and LLL-Canada. In one-day seminars, presenters Ian Adnams and Stephen Klinck provided congregations with practical communication strategies for print (church bulletins and newsletters), broadcast, and newspaper media. They also acquainted participants with other resources available through the Synod and LLL-Canada. In the early days of the program the seminar included information on congregations' need for computers and internet capability. Later the program was expanded to include information on establishing websites and email addresses as well as the use of internet and webpages for outreach. By 2004 almost 450 individuals representing 158 congregations and nine schools had participated in the training. A quick look at the number of LCC congregations with websites testifies to the success of this training program.

The "National Lutheran Open House" was another project of the Board for Communication Services with approximately half of LCC congregations participating. The goal of the program was to create awareness of the local congregation in their community and assist them in reaching out. LCC assisted in creating, producing, and acquiring resources for use in congregations. Thousands of DVD copies of the *Jesus* film were distributed as congregations held open houses, block parties, and other events in their community.

In 2007, the online outreach tool www.whatyoubelieve.ca was launched in connection with the National Lutheran Open House project. The page, attractively designed, began with a statement, "Everyone believes something," noting what you believe influences your life. The visitor was then asked to identify a topic of belief about God, Jesus, the Bible, life after death, or another subject. Clicking on a specific belief and statement would activate another screen which discussed the belief from a biblical perspective and then pointed out Scripture passages related to the topic. Visitors were invited to leave a response to the topic or be directed to other pages where they could ask a question or find a church or find out more on "what Lutherans believe." As data accumulated, it was shared with the church and with local congregations.

The Synod can be most thankful to God for the leadership of Ian Adnams in the area of communications. He was recognized for his leadership in the Synod by Concordia Lutheran Seminary in Edmonton, who awarded him an honorary doctorate in 2008.

***

Far more abundantly than all that we ask or think... in Synod structure.

Up to this point, this chapter has highlighted significant trends and events relating to the mission and ministry of the Synod. In this next section it is important to review the struggles that Synod had as it relates to its nature and structure. The word "struggle" is used deliberately as the Synod wrestled with the subject even before its formation. Various models were proposed and explored at conventions of the federated Lutheran Church–Canada (a federation of the three Canadian districts of The Lutheran Church—Missouri Synod), but there was no unanimity. It soon became obvious that if a national synod were to be formed, the church would have to adopt a structure and constitution with which everyone was familiar. The result was the adoption of a constitution reflecting that of the mother church, the LCMS.

It was recognized immediately that the structure and constitution adopted were cumbersome for a small synod about the size of some individual districts in the LCMS. In addition to a duplication of services between Synod and its districts, there were multiple layers of governance and organizational structure. While these did not appear to hinder the mission and ministry of Synod, the structure itself did not provide lines of accountability for program boards or for their staff because boards were accountable only to a national convention.

In 1990 the convention called upon the Commission for Constitutional Matters and Structure (CCMS) to consult with the districts and members of Synod regarding these concerns in a resolution, "To Restructure the Board of Directors." The CCMS reported at the following convention in 1993 that they could not make any recommendations since their consultations did not produce enough consensus among commission members. In response, the convention called for the formation of a "Task Force on the Nature and Structure of the Synod." The mandate given, as the name implies, was expanded to include the nature of Synod as well as its structure.

The task force, chaired by Mr. Walter Seehagel, after conducting multiple surveys and consultations, presented twenty recommendations to the 1996 convention. The following is a summary. The task force recommended a change in the nature of Synod with membership being held only by congregations. It also recommended that the Synod form districts—but these would serve as ministry regions, not as administrative units. District presidents would be elected by the national convention and serve as the vice-presidents of the Synod. All staff serving at the district level would be understood as being synodical staff and would be accountable to the synodical Board of Directors. The district presidents would in turn appoint Advisory Councils from their regions who would advise them on the ministry needs of their specific district. That input would contribute to the program and budget planning of the entire Synod. The report also recommended changing all boards of the Synod to committees accountable to the Board of Directors and through the Board of Directors to the Synod in convention. There was also a recommended change to the flow of funding. Congregational mission offerings would be directed to the Synod with a designated formula established for returning a portion to the districts to carry out their work.

The recommendations produced much debate at the convention, with strenuous opposition to some of the recommendations presented. In particular, objections were raised to the recommended changes in the nature of Synod and district structure. The latter were seen by delegates as simply an elimination of the three districts as regional administrative arms of the Synod. The result of the debate was the adoption of a resolution that recommended that the Board of Directors of Synod follow up on the Task Force report by consulting with districts, congregations, and rostered church workers, using the Task Force recommendations as "one" possible model for changes to the organizational structure of the Synod. It was also instructed to produce a final report for the next convention.

At the first meeting of the Board of Directors the resolution was assigned to the Commission on Constitutional Matters and Structure who subsequently appointed a committee to consider the matter. Following consultations, which basically reflected the debate that had taken place at the convention, the committee decided not to consider any changes to the structure of districts. That would wait for another day. They would instead centre their attention on the nature of Synod and its organizational structure. In so doing, the committee returned to the recommendations made at the 1990 convention.

Rather than present one resolution to the LCC 1999 Convention, the committee elected to present a series of seven resolutions. It was felt that in following this course, the delegates could more easily centre on a specific topic and the passing or defeat of a specific resolution would not necessarily impart other recommended changes.

Several resolutions were defeated. A resolution to change the membership of Synod to only congregations and pastors was defeated as was a resolution to combine Synod and district conventions with every congregation represented in a three-year cycle.

Adopted was a resolution that declared the Board of Directors as the decision-making body between conventions within the parameters of the constitution and bylaws of Synod. While the president remained accountable to Synod in convention in his role as president of Synod, as the Chief Executive Officer of the incorporated entity, Lutheran Church–Canada, he would be accountable to the Board of Directors. In turn, all synodical executive staff would be accountable to the president of Synod and through him to the Board of Directors.

While the voting membership of the Board of Directors remained essentially the same, the three district presidents were added as advisory members. It was felt that their addition would strengthen the relationship between Synod and its districts. The synodical Board of Directors would hear reports from each of the districts and the presidents in turn could report firsthand on the work of the Synod in their districts.

Another resolution centred on the establishment of a variety of Councils, Commissions, and Committees. The Council of Presidents would remain as previously constituted as would the Commission of Adjudication, the Committee on Constitutional Matters and Structure, and the Colloquy Committee. The Board of Directors would appoint one specific committee, the Committee for Missions and Social Ministry Services, which would now be accountable to the Board of Directors. The Board of Directors was also given the authority to appoint other committees as they felt needed: communications, coordinating council for parish services, and so forth. The Board of Higher Education was removed from the structure of Synod (to be replaced by a coordinating committee) as was the Board of Parish Services. The work of this Board was considered primarily a responsibility of each district.

One more resolution was proposed and adopted. It was a resolution tasking the Commission on Constitutional Matters and Structure with the responsibility of drafting the necessary constitutional and bylaw changes for implementation of the changes adopted and presenting them to the next convention of Lutheran Church–Canada.

The hard work was over. Now the detailed work of incorporating the adopted changes could begin. The Commission took up the challenge assisted by Synod's lawyer. In addition to the proposed amended constitution and bylaws, the Commission, upon the recommendation of Synod's lawyer, chose to add to the proposed documents the "Statutory Bylaws" to cement a connection between Synod and its incorporation in the Senate of Canada.

The Commission was now prepared to present the proposed Constitution and Bylaws as amended based on the adopted resolutions from the previous convention. Senior members of the Commission, remembering past conventions and the strenuous debate surrounding any resolutions related to structure, were concerned that ample time be given to delegates to ask questions and receive explanations. This was something not always possible in the normal course of convention debate.

Reflecting that concern and believing it is always best to be safe than sorry, it was proposed that we set aside time one evening of the convention as a kind of "committee of the whole" and have the chair of the Commission, Rev. Nolan Astley, walk the delegates through the documents, section by section, providing time for questions, explanations, and any proposals for changes that delegates might want to consider when the convention returned to a more formal debate, amendment, and vote. The convention approved the proposal.

From the Commission's perspective, the procedure was a blessing. Delegates had the chance to ask their questions, discuss their concerns, and even compare the proposed changes with the original documents. When debate began on the resolutions the following day, much of the discussion was completed. A few amendments were made as proposed the previous evening, and they were dealt with speedily. The convention was ready to vote, and the proposed amended Constitution and Bylaws were adopted.

Three significant changes were made that from my perspective were a blessing to Synod. The first was the establishment of the Board of Directors as the decision-making entity between conventions, limited only by the Constitution and Bylaws. The second was the establishment of a line of accountability for committees, synodical staff, and the president especially as it related to Synod as a corporate entity. The third was the changes reducing the number of boards and committees, especially in reference to the duplication of service. In redrafting the bylaws, some bylaws were removed noting that they more properly belonged in a board or committee manual.

***

Far more abundantly than all that we ask or think... in funding the mission.

One final area which needs to be highlighted as it proved to be a challenge relates to the funding of Synod and the changes in giving patterns. This challenge preceded my time of service. Already at the 1990 convention two resolutions were passed regarding funding. The first was a more general resolution calling upon the Board of Directors to develop and pursue alternate funding for the mission and ministry of Lutheran Church–Canada, emphasizing the biblical theology of stewardship. The second was more specific. Resolution 90:1.11 called upon the Board for Missions and Social Ministry Services to conduct a thorough study of "alternate methods of funding the mission activity of the Synod" including the formation of a mission society, direct solicitation for missions, personal mission support, and other appropriate methods.

A proposal was brought by the Board for Missions and Society Ministry Services to the Board of Directors of Synod following the 1993 convention to establish a Mission Society as a viable means to encourage mission awareness and support. The proposal was discussed and defeated. I must admit that I was one who voted against the proposal, joining others in thinking that the establishment of such an organization would impact the support given to the Synod as a whole. I regret that decision. It was short-sighted and did not give credence to the changes that were taking place in the giving patterns of God's people.

There was a time when people simply gave their "tithe" in worship and left the decision on how those gifts given were to be distributed to the congregation, the district, and the Synod. Those times were changing. Part of the reason for the change lay in the general change of attitude permeating our society. People were becoming less trustful of those in leadership and much more critical of the decisions being made. It was in our culture, and it was impacting the church.

A second reason can be tied to the rise in the educational level of our membership. (It is hard to imagine now that there were members in my first parish who could neither read nor write.) There was a growing desire on the part of God's people to be much more involved in the decision-making process. People viewed the present pattern as simply putting their gifts into a deep dark hole. They wanted much more information about what they were supporting. Some were interested in supporting a specific ministry or project that they could follow: a specific mission field or perhaps missionary, a specific seminary or social ministry program. Others became interested in becoming involved in the work of missions themselves. They were looking for "mission trip" experiences. In some cases, congregations, encouraged by their own members, were expressing an interest in taking on their own mission project separate from that of the district or Synod. The church needed to respond. At first that response appeared to be negative. The vote against the establishment of a mission society was a case in point. But the idea of a mission society did not die.

We can be thankful to God that He led President Emeritus Lehman to resurrect the proposal to establish a mission society soon after his retirement. In February 1997, he gathered a group of mission minded individuals from across the country in Winnipeg to discuss the feasibility of such a project. President Lehman described that meeting as being brutally honest as the challenges of starting such an organization were discussed. In the end, this group of mission minded individuals voted to take the leap of faith trusting that God would bless their labour and God did.

The name chosen was "Concordia Lutheran Mission Society."

It would be an independent society electing its own board, making its own decisions, and taking responsibility for those decisions. It would, however, not be disconnected from Synod. It would be an agency in support of Synod and its God-given mission. Its objectives were set out as follows: 1. Develop greater prayer support for and interest in missions; 2. Be involved in mission and stewardship education as it connects donors and ministry; 3. Generate financial support for mission work in Canada and abroad and cooperate with other mission agencies in funding projects; 4. Provide financial support and encouragement to missionaries throughout Canada and the world; 5. Assist the church in identifying prospective missionary personnel; and 6. Support mission opportunities which Lutheran Church–Canada may not be able to support.

The Board of Directors elected by the membership (all those who contribute to the society) would be a volunteer working board. All designated gifts to projects would be applied as requested, with no deductions for administrative costs. Administrative costs would be covered by gifts given specifically for that purpose. Requests to CLMS for funding would come from LCC's Board for Missions and Social Ministries, from the mission field itself, and from individuals who may have special knowledge of needs in the mission field. All proposed projects would be carefully evaluated based on a set of established criteria, with approved projects placed on a ballot to be voted upon at the annual meeting of the Board.

In its first year of operation, the Board established a goal of raising $6,900 in support of three projects, two in Ukraine and one in Southern Thailand. As of 2018, Concordia Lutheran Mission Society supported a total of 25 projects (two in Canada, thirteen in

Central America, eight in Ukraine, and one in South East Asia) for a total of $166,650 dollars. Lutheran Church–Canada can be most grateful to God for the financial support CLMS continues to give to the missions of our Synod, reaching out to mission-minded individuals in our congregations, acquainting them with the mission of the church, engaging them in prayer support, and giving them the opportunity to support specific mission projects of the Synod. The establishment of this mission agency has accomplished the goal set out in the original resolution passed in 1990, providing a way for "an individual donor to direct a financial contribution for the mission activity of the Synod and thus develop a sense of ownership in that mission." Soon after its establishment, CLMS was given the status of a "Listed Service Organization." In 2002 the Synod in Convention voted to give CLMS status as an "Auxiliary."

A final note in the discussion of alternate funding is the recent work of another agency of Synod: Lutheran Foundation Canada. While this agency under its formal name, Lutheran Church–Canada Financial Ministries, had existed in the handbook since the establishment of Synod, it was essentially dormant. The work assigned to it was already being carried out by the districts, with each district having its own boards and rules and regulations. This was one of the duplication of services discussed earlier.

In 2000-2001, the Central District began discussion with Synod about the possibility of transferring both their church extension and foundation to LCCFM. In preparation for such an amalgamation, the board of LCCFM felt it prudent to do some restructuring to better serve the Synod and its members, and so presented to the 2002 synodical convention a resolution "To revise the Synodical Bylaws regarding Lutheran Church–Canada Financial Ministries." The revision called for the establishment of LCCFM as a separate corporate entity within LCC, with each participating district entitled to be a member of the corporation. Each participating district (there were none at this point) would be entitled to two members on the board. The Synod would have three appointees, with the president of Synod and the treasurer serving as advisory members. The Board established as its mission the task of "empowering God's people to respond to His grace through gift planning." Their vision was to "envision the day when God's people, abundantly blessed, return His gifts in full measure to fund His work on earth," whether that be through the local congregation, district, Synod, or the many mission and service organizations that support the mission and ministry of LCC.

Discussions continued with the Central District with the result of those discussions leading to the transfer of the Central District Foundation to LCCFM. Around the same time, discussion also began with the Alberta-British Columbia District. They too made the decision to join and transferred their foundation to LCCFM. The East District, though not having a district foundation, also decided to become a member. Because each of the districts had different rules and regulations regarding their Church Extensions, the decision was made to leave the operation of the Church Extensions in the hands of the individual districts. The Board engaged the services of Gift Coordinators each working in a specific region. They would hold Christian Estate Planning Seminars in their regions and so make contacts with interested individuals.

God blessed their efforts. To date the foundation is aware of just over 63 million dollars in lifetime or estate gifts designated for congregations, for LCC, and for LCC-affiliated organizations. During this past year, 2018, a total of $196,000 was distributed. Having experienced the joy of giving in their lifetime, God's people are now being inspired to set aside a portion of the blessings received to establish a legacy for the mission and ministry of Christ's church in the years to come.

**

A personal note in closing

I give thanks to God for the privilege and opportunity He has given me to serve Christ and His church. It was a privilege to serve as president of Lutheran Church–Canada for twelve years, and I look back on those years with joy. But even more precious is the privilege I continue to have, and that is to share the Word of Christ with people, to pronounce the Word of Absolution in worship, and at the altar to consecrate and share with God's people the body and blood of Christ in the holy supper. What joy! What a privilege!

2008-2018

LUTHERAN CHURCH–CANADA

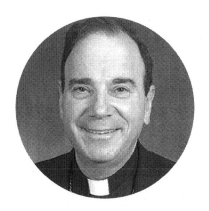

Robert Bugbee

Reflecting on an Honour:
My Years as Synodical President

S t. Paul wrote to his friends in 1 Corinthians 3:11-13: "For no one can lay a foundation other than that which is laid, which is Jesus Christ. Now if anyone builds on the foundation with gold, silver, precious stones, wood, hay, straw—each one's work will become manifest, for the Day will disclose it, because it will be revealed by fire, and the fire will test what sort of work each one has done."

The apostle teaches that we will not know the deepest way to understand or evaluate what any of us has done in the Lord's service until Christ's great day comes, when it will all be clear. Many things in which pastors and other Christian leaders took great pride will seem insignificant at that point as they are burned up and forgotten.

Other contributions, which people barely noticed, will sparkle before our wondering eyes.

It is important to remember those truths, both as I write and as others read and think about what I have written. I am not an historian in the professional sense. Since very little time has passed since I left office, I do not have the advantage of a long-term perspective on where my work fits into the overall history and development of Lutheran Church–Canada. It may be that my views on certain matters will seem very premature when I and others review my time in office in the more distant future.

From Parish to Presidency

In Bo Giertz's compelling story, *The Hammer of God*, a young assistant minister asks his superior, "Sir, can anything be greater than to be a pastor in God's church?"[1] I felt this very keenly through the years of my university and seminary education, and was still captivated by the glad blessing of serving Christ in that role through all the years He gave me as a pastor in local congregations.

When the Eighth LCC Convention, convened in Edmonton, Alberta in 2008, elected me to succeed the retiring President Ralph E. Mayan, I had been serving as the Senior Pastor of Holy Cross Lutheran Church at Kitchener, Ontario, for more than fourteen years. In the early years of my ministry, I had been involved with the church-at-large as a circuit counselor and a District Vice-President, but by 2008 had been focused already for quite some time on the work of our large congregation, where I functioned with multiple staff. Our parish, which had the distinction of providing stronger financial sup-

---

1   Giertz, Bo. *The Hammer of God*. Augsburg Publishing House, 1973: 225.

port to the church-at-large than any other Lutheran congregation in Canada, also had an independent streak and carried out many projects and ventures of its own. In some ways it was a microcosm of the overall landscape and even the struggles within the wider church. I had inherited the benefit of deep respect and support of the pastoral office in that congregation. This was largely due to the very faithful and steady work of my predecessor, Rev. Lloyd Wentzlaff, who had spent his entire pastoral ministry of 40 years in this one place.

I happened to be a voting pastoral delegate at the Eighth Convention, and was startled at how quickly the election process went. President Mayan and the delegates were very patient with the first limping remarks I made in response to their choice, and he invited me to the stage two days later to address them after I had collected my thoughts. The notes, emails, and spoken kindnesses in the early weeks and months impressed on me the good-heartedness of our people across the Synod. I came to realize later that all this was no accident. My predecessors in office, Edwin Lehman (1988-96) and Ralph Mayan (1996-2008), had laboured with that marvelous pastoral combination of doctrinal faithfulness and a willingness to work long and hard for God's people. As a result, the office of Synod President was held in high regard by many of our pastors and congregations.

This was the first time the Synod had elected a president from eastern Canada. Lehman and Mayan had both come to the job from the Alberta-British Columbia District. The chairman of the LCC Board of Directors, Randy Stefan, had very graciously offered that my installation festival and first round of meetings could take place that fall in Kitchener, so that many of those among whom I had worked and lived could participate. So, the installation festival "straddled" Church Street downtown, where our Synod's mother-church, Historic St. Paul's, stood across the street from the ELCIC's St. Matthew's with its large sanctuary. We rented the St. Matthew's nave, in which more than 500 people came to worship. Meanwhile Dr. Ian Adnams, the LCC Director of Communications, was in a side balcony providing video-streaming for another 100 "attendees" from across the country. Choirs from my Holy Cross congregation and the Kitchener-area Lutheran young adults were joined by gifted instrumentalists. Presidents Lehman and Mayan installed me in office, after which I took my place at the altar and installed the remaining leaders of the Synod. We returned to Historic St. Paul's afterward for a reception and celebrating. More than 70 pastors were vested and took part in the processional.

The next morning, it was right down to work! President Mayan remained for one hour to provide a wrap-up report from his administration, then shook my hand, wished me well, and off he went! The goodwill and patience of both the Board of Directors and the Council of Presidents were a precious treasure in those early days.

As we were in the throes of moving from Kitchener to Winnipeg, the news came that my wife, Gail, was diagnosed with advanced cancer. The regimen of treatments and surgeries facing her in a strange place made the adjustment challenging. But we were sustained by the constant prayer-support and love of our people across the church. The Lord turned back this threat to her life. As I write these lines nearly eleven years later, she is still beside me.

A Mari Usque ad Mare!

Canada's national motto from the old Latin Bible, "from sea to sea," is an ongoing reminder of the vastness of our country. But

Canada is markedly different from the United States, its neighbour to the south. We have more land and far fewer people... 37 million to their 327 million! In his days as a District president of The Lutheran Church—Missouri Synod, Edwin Lehman once described our challenge to the Americans next door: "Too few people in too much space!"

As I began my work in late 2008, LCC was indeed represented "from sea to sea," with its easternmost congregation at Dartmouth, Nova Scotia (since moved to Halifax), and its westernmost at Port Alberni on Vancouver Island in B.C. It would be a mistake for people to imagine that LCC congregations were well distributed throughout that expanse. It is more accurate to picture areas of concentration: in southern Ontario, Saskatchewan, Alberta, and the southern British Columbia mainland. In other regions, the LCC presence is far weaker: in the Maritimes, Quebec, northern Ontario, Manitoba, and the farther north one travels in British Columbia. Though a preaching station was launched in Prince Edward Island during my presidency, it has not developed into a strong congregation and, as far as I am aware, there is no Lutheran presence of any kind in Newfoundland. Meanwhile, Canada's north has been home to a very few ELCIC congregations in the Yukon and Northwest Territories, but Lutheran Church–Canada has planted no churches in that far-flung area.[2]

One early goal was to get better acquainted with areas and people I had not previously known. My first trips were focused on the two synodical Districts in Western Canada—that is, Central and Alberta-British Columbia—where about two-thirds of our national

2   Coincidentally, a member family of our First Lutheran Church (Windsor, Ontario) is currently stationed in Nunavut, which is emblematic of our situation: just a scattering of LCC people here and there in the far north, often only for a temporary period due to service with the RCMP or similar commitments.

membership was anchored. I made visits to Concordia University College of Alberta and Concordia Lutheran Seminary in Edmonton, as well as to the Boards of Directors of the two western Districts. I accepted preaching invitations to this part of the country whenever possible in those early years. The 2009 round of District conventions that spring got me to Vancouver for the first time, and provided an opportunity to connect with many of our key active lay people. Even more instructive were my encounters in local parishes, especially isolated ones which in some cases had not been visited by representatives of the national church. I had afternoon tea with two Cree grandmothers up north at Sucker River, Saskatchewan, a town served by our congregation at LaRonge, and was invited by Prime Minister Stephen Harper to a state dinner in the presence of Queen Elizabeth and Prince Philip at the Royal York Hotel in downtown Toronto. Ours is a gigantic land, diverse in many respects. It is also a land in need of the Good News of Jesus, especially in this time of change and confusion. The avenues open to our Synod to take that Good News into so many varied situations amazed me.

Mission Partners Abroad: Ukraine

I had been introduced to LCC's mission connections already in 1997 while serving at Holy Cross in Kitchener. Our congregation had ties to a Synodical missionary, Rev. Roland Syens, who served for some thirteen years at Dnepropetrovsk in eastern Ukraine. Rev. Syens made a number of visits to our church during those years, and members of our congregation served on short-term mission experiences in that country under his leadership. Meanwhile, the Synod's ties to Bishop Viktor Gräfenstein of the Synod of Evangelical

Lutheran Churches of Ukraine (SELCU) were deepening. President Mayan and Dr. Leonard Harms, LCC mission director at that time, had sent me to that former Soviet republic for a month in 1997 to gather information and provide reflections for our Canadian church.

In the years of my presidency, I made no less than six additional visits to Ukraine; these involved preaching in local parishes, observing the working of their annual convention, teaching at conferences of pastors and lay leaders, and participating in many fraternal conversations with Bishop Gräfenstein, his successor, Bishop Alexander Yurchenko, as well as with parish pastors. Beginning in 2007, Ukrainian students came for two-three year stays at our LCC seminaries: Rev. Oleg Schewtschenko in St. Catharines (now serving the SELCU congregation at Odessa), and Rev. Oleksiy Navrotskiy in Edmonton (now at the SELCU parish in Nikolayev). LCC's goal was never to lure young students or pastors away from their homeland, but rather to provide more advanced coursework and experience in the "ethos" of a Lutheran seminary in the hope of helping SELCU shape gifted servants for leadership in the future.

After many years of work and frequent construction delays, the Mission Centre building housing our Concordia Seminary was dedicated in the summer of 2010 at Usatovo, Ukraine, a northwest suburb of Odessa. LCC had assisted the SELCU with theological education after 1998, beginning in the village of Kamenka, about 40 kms northwest of Odessa. In the course of time, it was clear that ministry opportunities and a fuller shaping of future pastors would happen closer to the city. The Concordia Lutheran Mission Society (CLMS) poured significant financial support into the building venture. The seminary program was under the guidance of its Rector (President), Dr. Norman Threinen, who was still on the active faculty of Concordia Lutheran Seminary in Edmonton when this partnership began. He continued this work even after his retirement to British Columbia. After many years and countless visits to Ukraine, Dr. Threinen asked to be released from this commitment. He was succeeded by Dr. Wilhelm Torgerson, at that time a visiting professor at the seminary in St. Catharines. True to its historic missionary emphasis, the Regents and Faculty of CLS Edmonton continue to guide the Ukraine seminary program.

The SELCU, which began in 1996 with only Gräfenstein's congregation in Odessa, has grown meanwhile to include about thirteen local churches. They are located in the eastern and southern regions of the country, where the Russian language is more widely used than the official Ukrainian. One of the more distressing developments came in March 2014, when the Russian Federation under Vladimir Putin engineered the annexation of the Crimean peninsula. (The Soviet government had awarded Crimea to Ukrainian administration in 1954.) This gave rise to an armed boundary which separated five of the SELCU's congregations or preaching stations from the Ukrainian mainland. Crimean congregations continued to hold membership in SELCU, but the ties—evidenced by attendance at conventions and pastoral conferences—were weakened. Hostilities between Russia and Ukraine also made it difficult, for example, to transport Russian-language theological literature across the border from Russia to our Usatovo seminary, where resources are badly needed for its fledgling library.

Church relations in Ukraine have been challenging. Bishop Gräfenstein originally served in the German Evangelical Lutheran

Church of Ukraine (known by its German-language abbreviation, DELKU), but left it in the mid-1990s because of the theological influence of the German territorial (state) churches, which pushed for the ordination of women and other innovations that have caused much turmoil in certain segments of the Lutheran World Federation. In fact, after Gräfenstein's departure to the SELCU, bishops for the DELKU were generally sent in from Germany.

This changed during my presidency when the DELKU elected its first Ukrainian-based bishop, Rev. Sergej Maschewski. Bishop Maschewski had actually studied for several years in the Russian program of The Lutheran Church—Missouri Synod's seminary at Fort Wayne, and brought a more biblical and confessional emphasis to the DELKU. He also cultivated ties to the Missouri Synod, which ended up entering Ukraine without advance consultation with LCC. The story is long and complicated, but certain elements of the DELKU rebelled against Maschewski, causing a major split in that church. Personal and church relations difficulties have added to the strain, so that the present situation is marked by confusion and discord. Our LCC involvement with SELCU and the Usatovo seminary was still strong at the time I left office in early 2018, for which I thank God.

Mission Partners Abroad: Central America

The Lutheran Church Synod of Nicaragua (*Iglesia Luterana Sínodo de Nicaragua – ILSN*) was founded and became self-governing toward the close of President Ralph Mayan's tenure. He and Dr. Leonard Harms had worked hard to send the first LCC missionary to Nicaragua, and to guide this emerging partner toward greater maturity. LCC also provided theological education to the fledgling church at the mission centre in the city of Chinandega. Even beyond the training of pastors, an impressive program of deaconess education took place there. Large numbers of deaconesses provided the backbone of the children's education program which went on multiple days each week in virtually every ILSN congregation, and they were often the first contacts between the church and newcomers, especially as non-member parents sent their children to classes in villages where the ILSN was represented.

Meanwhile the ILSN reached across national boundaries in both directions and began to include mission stations in neighbouring Costa Rica and in Honduras. The visits I made to Central America during my time in office took me to a number of local congregations in Nicaragua and Honduras, where I was able to witness not only the regular worship of the members but also the children's classes and the impressive children's feeding program, for example, in the Nicaraguan village of Rancheria. In those days the sewing school was still active on the mission centre campus, and space was set aside for the much sought-after medical clinic on the same site.

Numerous LCC congregations and people have traveled for short-term mission trips to Nicaragua over the years, providing staffing for VBS-style programs and assisting with the construction and enhancement of chapels for worship. Our St. Catharines Seminary has taken a strong role in providing theological education in Chinandega. Meanwhile, Lutheran Hour Ministries (which has the status of an "Auxiliary" in LCC) has a field office in León, Nicaragua. I participated in the dedication of their new building in the later years of my tenure.

The first ILSN President, Rev. Luis Turcios of Chinandega, was succeeded at their 2012 Convention by Rev. Marvin Donaire, who had been serving a rural three-point parish. Under President Donaire, the ILSN became acquainted with the International Lutheran Council (ILC) and its Latin American region. The ILC World Conference in 2015 at Buenos Aires, Argentina, voted to accept the ILSN as a full member church body.

Political turmoil in Nicaragua began affecting our partners there adversely around the time I left office. Because of the violence and shooting deaths in some places, we were advised as foreign nationals to suspend our visits and direct involvement for a time. Resumption of the numerous contacts and visits is fervently to be hoped and prayed for, above all for the sake of the peace and security of our church members, pastors, and deaconesses there.

By mutual agreement, LCC's work in Honduras was shifted to The Lutheran Church—Missouri Synod in 2018. The pioneers of the emerging Honduran national church, Deacon Tulio Meza of Tegucigalpa and Rev. Junior Martinez of LaPaz, both received their theological training at our ILSN seminary in Chinandega.

Our Synod was blessed that President Ralph Mayan continued to work as our interim mission executive after he left the presidency in 2008. That position had become vacant already in President Mayan's tenure with the retirement of Dr. Leonard V. Harms. Mayan had not filled the vacancy, primarily out of consideration for whomever the Synod would choose to succeed him, so that the incoming Synod president could be involved in the choice of a new mission executive. Mayan looked after the mission portfolio part-time at the end of his last term, and continued to do this work during the first year of his "retirement" from his new home in Langley, B.C. In 2009 the LCC Board of Directors extended a call to Dr. Leonardo Neitzel, a native of Brazil, who at that time was pastor of Bethlehem Lutheran Church in Vancouver. Dr. Neitzel had served on the faculty of the mission seminary of our Brazilian partner church in São Paulo, and had been a mission developer in his homeland. Neitzel's facility in Spanish as well as Portuguese were a welcome asset as he guided our mission program in Central America. Meanwhile, even after handing off the mission portfolio to Neitzel, Dr. Mayan continued to make repeated lengthy visits every year to the mission centre in Nicaragua. Our colleagues in the Nicaraguan church saw him much as I did, as a true "Barnabas," offering fatherly wisdom and encouragement to an emerging church amid its growing pains.

My repeated visits to Nicaragua revealed a very unique religious landscape. As a Spanish-speaking country, the land has a strong Roman Catholic heritage. One notices impressive Catholic churches and cathedrals in larger cities. The rural areas tell a different story. Many, if not most, smaller villages are not served by the Roman Church in any active way. Because Nicaragua is one of the poorest countries of the western hemisphere, the rural people often have neither the means nor the money to attend Catholic masses in the urban centres. As a result, numerous Protestant and evangelical fellowships have poured into the countryside, as have religious groups like the Jehovah's Witnesses. Our ILSN congregations have tended to be a presence in smaller towns and villages. One of the ILSN's primary concerns—shared also by the Lutheran Hour Ministries people in León—is the planting of biblical Lutheran congregations in cities like the national capital, Managua.

Mission Partners Abroad: Southeast Asia

Not only did we benefit from Dr. Mayan's continued involvement in Nicaragua well into retirement, but the Synod's former mission executive, Dr. Leonard Harms, fulfilled a very similar role in southeast Asia. He and his wife, Carole, maintained a modest apartment in Bangkok for a number of years into my presidency.

Our work in southeast Asia focused largely on Thailand and Cambodia. Though they are neighbours geographically, the two countries display marked differences. Thailand had its British influences—including driving in the left lane on the roads!—and seemed one of the more stable countries in the region under King Rama IX, who reigned for 70 years until his death in 2016. LCC's early mission partners in the Phuket region of southern Thailand became part of a merger known as the Thailand Concordia Lutheran Church (TCLC) under its President, Rev. Pornprom "Ted" NaThalang. TCLC even included some people in the northern reaches of Thailand who had earlier missionary connections with the Wisconsin Synod. Lutheran Hour Ministries was also active in the country and maintained an office in Bangkok. Some challenges in the early years of the merged church developed precisely because it was a merger involving people with different backgrounds and associations. In addition, President NaThalang maintained residences both in Thailand and in the United States, and so was not able to give full-time involvement to those under his care.

An agency with much influence in those days was the Luther Institute Southeast Asia (LISA), which sought to provide theological training in various places throughout the region. Dr. Harms was active, both on the governing board of LISA and as a theological instructor. Following an invitation to Phom Penh, Cambodia, Harms began making teaching visits there, initially offering lectures on Luther's Small Catechism, as well as on the Augsburg Confession.

Political and churchly developments in Cambodia were markedly different from Thailand. A former French colony, Cambodia had suffered extensively under the Pol Pot regime with large-scale torture and the murder of tens of thousands. As I understood it, any public expression of Christian faith was prohibited into the early 1990s. The Christian churches bore the marks of this oppression. For one thing, the churches had existed as a largely underground movement during the most difficult phase of the persecution. In addition, there was no extensive network, and many congregations worked independently without any synodical or denominational ties. Theologically, they tended to be conservative in the sense that they took a high view of biblical authority and inspiration, as churches trying to cope with repression often do. But they lacked an overarching theological approach, and had survived as best they could without the presence of deeper pastoral training.

Pastors and others who attended Harms' initial lectures in Cambodia were therefore representatives of independent congregations, generally speaking. They responded very positively to the confessional Lutheran theology offered in his teaching. It must have been an emotional experience for him at the end of his lectures one day to witness his students gathering in a corner of the room around a table and resolving on their own initiative to found the Evangelical Lutheran Church of Cambodia (ELCC).

By contrast with Thailand, the Cambodian church expanded

rapidly. In the latter years of my presidency, they numbered over 30 primary congregations, many of which reached out into isolated areas near them to form a network of no less than 156 preaching stations. The very gifted and energetic president in those early years was Rev. Vannarith Chhim, whom I met on two visits to Cambodia, and who attended the Tenth LCC Convention in Vancouver in 2014. Within a year after that, the sorrowful news came that President Vannarith would resign the ministry because of moral and ethical problems in his life. The church leadership struggled to pick up the pieces, since too much of their function had been dependent on the former president. Since the ELCC's government registration had also expired, various considerations made it actually necessary to let the church's registration lapse and to reconstitute the entire effort under a new name: the Cambodia Lutheran Church.

Canadian Lutheran World Relief

Though we generally referred to our colleagues Harms and Neitzel as "mission executives," the formal title of the position they held was "Assistant to the President—Mission and Social Ministry Services." While both of them focused heavily on moving international mission activity forward, their work on the social ministry side took place in partnership with Canadian Lutheran World Relief (CLWR).

CLWR was organized by Lutherans in Canada after the Second World War, largely to assist refugees and displaced persons to find a new home in our country. By the time I came to office, it was a very sophisticated agency working in many areas of world relief and human care. CLWR related formally to the two larger Lutheran bodies in Canada, our LCC and the Evangelical Lutheran Church in Canada.

The ELCIC's Bishop, Susan Johnson, sat as an advisory member of the CLWR Board of Directors, as I also did. The voting make-up of the CLWR Board was proportional to the size of its participating churches. CLWR's Executive Director during my entire tenure was a very able ELCIC layman from Winnipeg, Robert Granke.

Those who know our church's story for the 30 years following World War II will know that inter-Lutheran relationships grew and deepened during that period. The Lutheran Council in Canada (LCIC) had a large office in Winnipeg with full-time staff persons. By the mid-1970s, it became clear that the hoped-for pan-Lutheran merger of all three major church bodies in Canada would not take place, primarily because of disagreements over the ordination of women and the inspiration and authority of Holy Scripture. The diverging approaches to the Scripture question, moreover, would give rise to sharply differing positions on many other matters, including communion fellowship, abortion, and ultimately on marriage and human sexuality. As a result, LCIC was sharply scaled down, and generally met only briefly once a year during my presidency, focusing on very few matters, such as military chaplaincy, federal prison chaplaincy, and the scouting movement.

This meant that CLWR was the primary regular point of contact between LCC and ELCIC after the 1980s. Because of its extensive ties with the Canadian government and agencies like the Canadian Foodgrains Bank, CLWR had a wide social ministry reach in many parts of the world. Many of its foreign projects were carried out with social ministry units of the Lutheran World Federation. Though LCC had no eucharistic fellowship with the ELCIC or most LWF member churches, these projects were generally seen as cooperation in externals. In addition, CLWR supported a number of church-specific projects each year, and under that provision provided funding especially for our work in Nicaragua, particularly for its medical and dental missions, and for the extensive children's education program going on in ILSN congregations.

Because of the growing number of refugees throughout the world, CLWR determined to focus again more strongly on that concern as it had originally done after its founding. In an attempt to "practice what we preach," the Winnipeg office staffs of CLWR, ELCIC, and LCC jointly raised funds to sponsor a young couple from Syria, Ahmad Al-Khattab and his wife, Khadija Moghrabi, with their two sons. I shall never forget the evening in late February 2016, when a number of us gathered at the Winnipeg airport to welcome these newcomers to Canada. Down the escalator they came on their way to the baggage carousel, and after the customary polite greetings, Ahmad asked me, "Is it cold outside?" Apparently, he had heard something about Winnipeg. I replied, "Actually, for this time of year and this part of Canada, it's not too bad ... -9 Celsius, I think." He bravely made his way out the door into the winter night, and into a new life. It was heart warming to witness the industry, frugality, and gratitude of these new Canadians as they put down roots in a new homeland.

LCC in the International Lutheran Council

Originally organized as a loosely-constituted "conference" of confessional Lutheran church bodies, the ILC grew and solidified its work during my tenure. In the early 1990s, the ILC redefined itself as a "council" (as opposed to an occasional "conference"), and by 2018 became an incorporated entity. The early leaders of LCC enjoyed the confidence of many ILC churches and people. As one of them once told me, "LCC is well-established enough to understand the large member churches like the Missouri Synod, and yet small enough to understand us who often have to struggle in our corners of the world." This confidence became concrete when both my predecessors, Lehman and Mayan, served for a time as elected Chairman of the ILC. Throughout my presidency I had the honour of sitting on the ILC's Executive Committee as the North American area representative. At the time I left office, I expected that my ILC involvement would be over, but the Executive Committee required an additional member when the Council became legally incorporated, and asked me to continue in this special capacity.

As the twenty-first century began to unfold, there had been increasing tensions within the large Lutheran World Federation, much of it focusing on the decision of some of its member churches—like the ELCA, ELCIC, and the Church of Sweden—to normalize same-gender relationships and to ordain those living in such relationships to the Holy Ministry. To be sure, the disagreements on human sexuality were really a symptom of deeper divisions on the authority and normative character of the Bible. Some of the largest and most rapidly growing Lutheran church bodies are located in the Global South, where some number many millions of members, particularly in places like Ethiopia, Tanzania, and Madagascar. Some of these church bodies had long-standing ties with LWF member churches, because missionaries from those churches were often the ones who had planted Lutheran groups in Africa. At the same time, the general persuasion of the African churches was far more conservative in theological and moral questions than established Lutheran churches in Western Europe and North America. At the same time, the growing African church bodies were highly dependent on financial and other forms of concrete support from the LWF and its affiliates.

The challenge of "dual membership" had stood between the ILC and the LWF for a number of decades. This happened in some cases because church bodies organized under the influence of Missouri Synod missionaries had decided to join the LWF, though did not wish to sever their ties with the ILC. The ILC freely acknowledged and permitted this situation. It did cause some irregularities, since the LWF increasingly defined itself as a "communion of churches," with the understanding that membership in the LWF, by definition, placed a church in communion with all their other members. There were dual membership churches who clearly did not understand themselves to be in such full communion.

Later, Ethiopia's Evangelical Church Mekane Yesus—which has grown to become the largest Lutheran church body in the world—in a very formal and public way severed its fellowship with the ELCA and the Church of Sweden because of their actions relating to same-gender relationships. It is perhaps not surprising that representatives of African groups have taken up contact with the ILC or directly with The Lutheran Church—Missouri Synod and have formed partnerships of various kinds. These and related issues moved the LWF to suspend its regular annual meetings with ILC representatives. As of this writing, the way forward for the ILC and LWF to relate to one another is unclear.

Roman Catholic Dialogues
in Canada and the World

Dialogue began rather simply. Dr. John Stephenson of our St. Catharines Seminary became personally acquainted with the Roman Catholic bishop of St. Catharines, Gerard Bergie. The initial friendly contacts between them gave rise to the proposal that twice-annual dialogue meetings be launched between LCC and the Canadian Conference of Catholic Bishops (CCCB). These meetings received the express authorization of both CCCB and the LCC's Commission on Theology and Church Relations (CTCR). For reasons of good stewardship, the original representatives were from southern Ontario, and tended to meet in St. Catharines, an easy drive for most participants. This national dialogue resulted in an invitation to me to address the full CCCB at its annual plenary meeting in September 2016, at Cornwall, Ontario. More than one participant at that meeting seemed pleasantly surprised to learn that there was more than one "camp" of Lutherans in the world, and to find out that our Synod and its affiliates have been grateful for the Roman Catholic witness, especially on the sanctity of unborn life and traditional marriage.

To be sure, serious theological differences continue to separate our churches. This brings up one of the characteristics exhibited by the Roman Catholic representatives to our common dialogue. The conversations were unfailingly polite and collegial. At the same time, the Catholic participants felt as ours did, that truth must not be compromised, and that one's theological convictions should be honestly stated and not muffled merely for the sake of "getting along." I expressed appreciation for this integrity when I addressed the Catholic bishops in Cornwall.

Meanwhile, the former president of Concordia University College of Alberta, Dr. Gerald Krispin, worked with the office of Archbishop Smith in Edmonton to launch a more regional series of dialogue meetings for their part of the country. Our CTCR also gladly supported this effort, which continued even after President Krispin left the ministerium of the Synod.

These LCC-based initiatives actually pre-dated a similar effort launched by the ILC in cooperation with the Pontifical Council for Promoting Christian Unity (PCPCU) under Cardinal Kurt Koch. In the fall of 2013, I was one of four ILC representatives who met Cardinal Koch and his assistant at the Vatican to discuss this possibility. The next year the early meetings began, largely made up of theologians based in Germany, though LCC had the honour of "lending" Dr. John Stephenson to become a member of this so-called "informal" dialogue.

Relationships Fading and Growing

As mentioned previously, the inter-Lutheran landscape in Canada in the decades after the Second World War was marked by convergence. Various church bodies which had no history of work in common were "thrown together" by the social ministry and military chaplaincy demands of the war and its aftermath.

By the 1960s, most Lutheran congregations in Canada held membership in one of three church bodies: Lutheran Church in America—Canada Section (LCA), by some measurements the most progressive (or "liberal") of the three, a division of its American parent, with headquarters in New York; the Evangelical Lutheran Church of Canada (ELCC), formerly the Canada District of The American Lutheran Church, which had gained autonomy from the American body in 1967; and Lutheran Church–Canada (LCC), the federation of districts of The Lutheran Church—Missouri Synod, certainly the most conservative of the three. While the LCA was very strong in eastern Canada and traced its roots to the earliest Lutherans in our country, the ELCC had its strength in the Canadian prairies, with only a handful of congregations east of the Great Lakes. The ELCC developed, among others, from predecessor groups of the ALC with a very strong confessional tradition, notably the Ohio Synod, as well as from Norwegian groups which were fairly pietistic and conservative. While LCA and ELCC were in fellowship, there was much in the ELCC's "DNA" which gave it an affinity for LCC pastors and people, perhaps most of all in Saskatchewan.

Up to the 1970s, hopes ran high that all three of these bodies would succeed in doing what was unimaginable in the United States—namely, to create one united major Lutheran Church. However, some of the same theological struggles that caused division within The Lutheran Church—Missouri Synod and between the Missouri Synod and other churches proved disruptive in Canada also. By 1977, it was clear that a three-way merger would not take place. From that point on, as LCC slowly moved toward autonomy, the others—LCA and ELCC— moved toward a two-way merger, which took place in 1986. That year marked the creation of the new "Evangelical Lutheran Church in Canada" (ELCIC). Shortly thereafter followed LCC's constituting convention in 1988 in Winnipeg, and the primary relationship between LCC and the ELCIC became bilateral.

It seemed clear to both church bodies that, as the years went by, their courses were not only different, but diverging even further. Whether the issue was the ordination of women, admission to Holy Communion, the extent of ecumenical involvement, abortion, or same-gender relationships, the two groups tended to come to opposing conclusions. To be sure, all these symptoms grew from a more basic disconnect, that is, the churches' understanding of the nature, inspiration, and authority of Scripture. Even the understanding and use of words like "Gospel" and "Evangelical" took on a different slant in the course of time.

Following the decision of the Evangelical Lutheran Church in America (ELCA) to legitimize same-gender relationships and to provide for the ordination of same-gender candidates to the ministry in 2009, the ELCIC followed suit in 2011. This caused the departure of hundreds of ELCA congregations from its membership in the ensuing years, and of dozens from the ELCIC. Though Lutheran Church–Canada took no pleasure in voicing public criticism of the ELCIC, our Council of Presidents did issue a statement on Same-Gender Relationships among Lutherans in Canada in the aftermath of the ELCIC's 2011 Convention. LCC's concern at that point was to prevent the impression among the larger Canadian public that all Lutherans in Canada were departing from the historic Christian understanding of marriage.

Aside from the regular contacts the two churches had through CLWR and the very infrequent meetings of the Lutheran Council in Canada, there were no efforts at theological dialogue throughout my presidency. Judging from the impressions I received even at informally "floating" the possibility, there was no serious interest on either side. Both churches seemed to sense that the distance between them had become too great, and that theological discussions would be a poor use of time. It was certainly clear that, even if these churches had at one time been each other's primary partners, this was no longer the case. Both of them were clearly motivated to invest greater time and energy into their current partnerships. In the case of the ELCIC, this would involve the ELCA, the Lutheran World Federation, and the Anglican Church of Canada (ACC). For LCC it involved The Lutheran Church—Missouri Synod and the International Lutheran Council.

While a growing distance set in between LCC and ELCIC, the sexuality decisions of the ELCA in 2009 and the ELCIC in 2011 unexpectedly opened new relationships. Lutheran pastors and congregations who feared the impending decisions began reaching out to us. Some of those involved in a doctrinal concerns movement in the ELCIC invited me to meetings in Alberta involving also the Canadian Association of Lutheran Congregations (CALC). After the ELCIC decision caused a number of them to leave their church body and to seek new associations, we had already established good rapport with them.

In December 2011, President Matthew Harrison of The Lutheran Church—Missouri Synod invited representatives of the new North American Lutheran Church (NALC) to come to St. Louis for get-acquainted talks. The NALC had been organized by people who had left the ELCA, largely because of its sexuality decisions. Since the NALC would ultimately also include congregations in Canada who departed the ELCIC, I was invited to participate also. Out of this grew a regular series of semi-annual meetings conducted by LCMS, NALC, and LCC. The LCC Worker Benefit Plans also expressed its willingness to enrol NALC pastors and congregations who had been left without such coverage, since it was unlikely that the NALC would be able to offer this service to its Canadian members, at least for a time. LCC representatives have also repeatedly attended the NALC's annual conventions, and the three church bodies—LCMS, NALC, and LCC—published a joint statement on Holy Scripture in 2016. Though the NALC on the one hand and LCMS/LCC on the other still hold different positions on women's ordination and Holy Communion practice, the discussions are marked by a very collegial spirit, and there is a profound respect for God's Word and a desire for theological and confessional integrity.

Somewhat parallel to these inter-Lutheran developments came contacts from the Anglican communion. The theological development of The Episcopal Church (TEC) in the U.S. and the Anglican Church of Canada (ACC) could legitimately be compared to that in Lutheran bodies like ELCA and ELCIC. Once again, the disruptive issues of human sexuality caused a growing number of Episcopalians in the United States and Anglicans in Canada to withdraw from their long time church homes and to create something new. Thus was founded the Anglican Church in North America (ACNA), which also has a Canadian subdivision known as the Anglican Network in Canada (ANiC). Similar to the LCMS/NALC/LCC dialogues, there emerged a regular series of ACNA/LCMS/LCC conversations twice each year. One of the senior members of this group is Dr. John Stephenson of our St. Catharines Seminary, who was reared in England and in Anglicanism and later came by conviction into confessional Lutheran circles. These dialogues revealed a remarkable commonality on many theological questions, and an interim report, *On Closer*

Acquaintance, was published by the three churches in 2016.

In the aftermath of my leaving office, the ACNA/LCMS/LCC discussions seemed to be paving a path toward more global contacts between the Global Anglican Future Conference (GAFCON)—a biblical Anglican fellowship of churches and bishops—and our International Lutheran Council. So even as some of our former associations seemed to be fading, the Lord brought us closer to confessing Christians who are serious about Holy Scripture, committed to the biblical Gospel of Jesus Christ as the hope of a lost humanity, and eager to live under Christ and His Word in their personal and churchly lives.

Pastors with Alternate Training (PAT)

I was not involved in synodical administration at the time of the convention which authorized the program known as "Pastors with Alternate Training" (PAT). As I came to understand, it was designed to meet two needs. First, it meant to provide pastoral presence in isolated parts of Canada where a gifted layman in the congregation might study for the ministry but would be prevented from attending one of our LCC seminaries, since the isolated congregation could fade or even wither away during his absence. Second, it could provide pastoral presence in certain ethnic communities where a language barrier or the lack of academic prerequisites could keep an acknowledged layman from enrolling at the seminary, not to mention threaten the well-being of the fledgling ethnic congregation during his years of study.

Although some segments of the Synod were concerned that the PAT program might create a "second track" toward ordination that could have the effect of hurting seminary enrolment or depriving the Synod of thoroughly trained pastors, the PAT program did not result in a huge number of new candidates bypassing the traditional route to the Holy Ministry. In fact, nearly a decade went by before we ordained our first PAT candidate, Rev. Asefa Aredo, who as of this writing is pastor of the Oromo congregation in Winnipeg. Rev. Aredo's ordination was followed by several others in the ensuing years. Efforts were made to involve our seminaries in the delivery of theological training to the PAT candidates, and the men ordained during my presidency impressed me as sincere servants of Christ who wanted to be loyal to the Scriptures, our confessions, and the doctrinal positions of the Synod.

Central District Move

The Synod's Central District covered a large area, from Nipigon, Ontario in the east to Maple Creek, Saskatchewan in the west—nearly 1,800 kms via the Trans-Canada highway. Prior to LCC autonomy, the area was not quite so extensive, since the former Manitoba and Saskatchewan District of the Missouri Synod basically took in just the two provinces. Congregations in northwestern Ontario had been tied to the LCMS Minnesota North District. The addition of these Ontario congregations was a glad blessing, and the name-change clearly made sense. Like the Synod as a whole, the Central District's member congregations were not at all evenly distributed across the full area it served. A strong majority of them were within the province of Saskatchewan. This may be part of the reason why the District office was moved many years ago to a converted private home at 1927 Grant Drive in Regina.

District President Thomas Prachar reported that there were

structural problems with that building. The District explored the possibility of constructing a new headquarters as well as a building project in conjunction with a Regina-area congregation to see whether shared premises might be a solution. For various reasons the idea proved unworkable. Thus, the Synod and Central District consulted about the possibility of moving the District's administrative offices to the LCC's own building on Portage Avenue in Winnipeg. Under this arrangement, the Synod would provide support staff, for which the District would reimburse the national church. The idea was ultimately approved by the Central District's Board of Directors, and the move took place in March 2013. Lil Kozussek, a long time employee of LCC, was assigned to provide the primary staff support to President Prachar. Chapel and meeting room spaces were henceforth used by both entities, a better use of facilities from a stewardship point of view. Soon David Friesen of Winnipeg took up his work in the building as the Central District's planned giving counselor for Lutheran Foundation Canada.

Church Extension Fund Crisis in the West

It would be difficult in a brief space to do justice to one of the most sorrowful developments in LCC history: the failure of the Church Extension Fund (CEF) of the Alberta-British Columbia (ABC) District. It is also challenging because, as of this writing, the matter remains before the courts, so that the very final chapters of the story have yet to be written.

The CEF program had been deeply supported by members and congregations in the ABC District, and had grown in assets beyond those in the other Districts. Unlike the Central District, which had actually restructured its CEF to become separately incorporated from the District itself, ABC continued to administer its Church Extension Fund as a department of the District corporation.

The primary challenge to the ABC CEF came through its involvement in the Prince of Peace complex just outside the eastern boundary of the city of Calgary. Prince of Peace Lutheran Church, which had existed for years within the city, was relocated to a new tract of land which was developed not only for the congregation, but also for a new Lutheran elementary school, for retirement condominiums and bungalows, and the like. Ultimately agreements were reached with Alberta Health for the construction of a dementia care centre. Construction difficulties, water supply challenges, and other financial problems surfaced in the course of time.

In January 2015, ABC District President Donald Schiemann wrote to the hundreds of CEF account holders that there was a significant challenge. It involved also the agency known as District Investments Limited (DIL). In fact, the financial shortfalls facing the CEF and DIL were beyond the District's ability to handle. Because the CEF was not a separate entity from the District, the CEF's insolvency meant that the District was insolvent, too.

The District leadership initially hoped that this challenge could be handled on a more informal basis between the District and its creditors. When this became impossible, the District filed for protection under the Companies' Creditors Arrangement Act (CCAA). The District's operations were placed under a court-appointed Monitor which had control of the District's expenditures. The understandable goal was that the District's assets should be protected so that they could be repaid to the account-holders as fully as possible. Even the mission remittances that LCC congregations in Alberta and British Columbia had sent to the District with the understanding that a portion of them be forwarded to the national church for its work were frozen. Soon a number of ABC District congregations began sending those remittances directly to the Synod in Winnipeg so that they could be used in keeping with their original intent.

A large part of the challenge for the Synod in those days was the fact that Lutheran Church–Canada and its Districts were separately incorporated entities. While the Districts for spiritual and ecclesiastical purposes were divisions of the Synod, the Districts as corporations were as distinct from Lutheran Church–Canada as, say, the TD Bank is from the Bank of Montreal. It would not have been legal, for example, for LCC to behave as a "head office" which could seize control of the District as a "branch office" and demand changes. Even active members of congregations often did not realize that, for example, the District Church Extension Funds were not mere branches of one and the same entity.

In the months following announcement of this crisis, I addressed pastoral letters to LCC pastors and people in Alberta and British Columbia in an attempt to take their pain very seriously, even though LCC as a corporate entity could not intervene. The spring of 2015 brought the customary round of District conventions, though it was clear that the ABC District convention would be anything but "routine" or "customary" in light of the trauma the District was facing. The District leadership felt constrained to simplify the convention by moving it away from its original planned venue at a Calgary hotel, and scheduled its sessions on the campus of Prince of Peace Lutheran School, which had been the focus of many people's concern and criticism.

In the lead-up to that convention, Lutheran Church–Canada felt strongly that a clear distinction had to be made between the spiritual and the corporate. A resolution was ultimately presented that, for a time, the District convention delegates should request the Synod president to appoint what became known as an "interim pastoral leader" to assume the spiritual functions of the District president until some of the legal and corporate challenges had run their course. Such a leader would be able to address the sorrows and struggles of pastors and members of congregations without having to deal with the legal challenges of the District corporation. Likewise, the man to be elected as District president would be free to address the corporation's considerable legal and financial problems.

I spoke very clearly in favour of the proposal. Although the voting took place by a show of hands, it was clear that at least 90 percent of the delegates voted for adoption. I ultimately appointed the Synod's First Vice-President, Rev. Nolan D. Astley, to assume the role of Interim Pastoral Leader for LCC congregations in Alberta and British Columbia. Rev. Astley had succeeded me in 2009 as Senior Pastor of Holy Cross Lutheran Church, Kitchener, Ontario, and had not had any involvement in ABC District administration. At the same time, he hailed originally from Edmonton and had spent the first 24 years of his ministry in the ABC District. He thus had a deep familiarity with congregations, pastors, and many of the leading lay people of that segment of the Synod. I was heartened when the members of Holy Cross voted very selflessly to share their pastor with our people in western Canada at that time of need. Rev. Astley continued this work for approximately a year.

Meanwhile, President Schiemann had already announced his decision to retire. The 2015 ABC District convention elected the District's mission executive, Rev. Dr. Glenn E. Schaeffer, to succeed him. Rev. Astley and President Schaeffer were installed that fall in a joint service into this now divided range of responsibilities.

Concordia University College of Alberta

This institution has been known by various names since it was founded nearly a century ago. It was for many years "Concordia College," one of the Missouri Synod's small regional schools scattered across North America, which had as one of its central purposes the preparation of pastors and parochial school teachers for service in the church. During my years at Concordia Seminary in St. Louis, I came to know Dr. Alfred Rehwinkel, one of the early fathers of the college in Edmonton. After his years in western Canada, Dr. Rehwinkel ended up on the St. Louis Seminary faculty until his retirement. By the time I came to know him he was a widower in his early nineties. St. Louis students had vowed to keep him out of a nursing home by moving into his apartment, taking turns looking after him with other seminarians. When he heard I would come as a summer intern to serve the congregation at Medicine Hat, Alberta, I remember him brightening considerably and saying, "Jetzt kommen Sie ins Paradies!" ("Now you're going to enter paradise!")

My 1978 summer sojourn in Medicine Hat included also my first visit to Edmonton, where I came to know another of Concordia College's formative leaders, Dr. Albert Schwermann, by then living in retirement in Edmonton. The affection between our churches in western Canada and that institution was clear just from the way in which these honoured fathers spoke. The college had certainly experienced its ups and downs over the years, but it was a well-established and respected institution when I came to the Synod Presidency in late 2008. By then it was known as "Concordia University College of Alberta" (CUCA), and had Rev. Dr. Gerald S. Krispin as its President. Dr. Krispin was a very learned and articulate confessional Lutheran theologian. He also had the challenging task of balancing the school's commitment to its Lutheran Christian heritage with the pressures that come with high levels of public funding. In addition, the majority of students and faculty came from outside the ranks of our church, and thus the atmosphere on campus was obviously very different from the time of Rehwinkel and Schwermann.

When CUCA's governing board felt constrained to expand its membership to include many people from outside the church, the understandable reason given was that the school needed to survive in the very competitive secondary education market in the province of Alberta, and thus required members well connected to the Edmonton area and various potential donors. Though a number of us in the Synod felt uneasy about this, I took comfort in the repeated assurances given me by President Krispin that the church had a "mission/vision/values statement" into which the Christian heritage and outlook were hard-wired.

By 2015, the school's title had changed again, this time to "Concordia University of Edmonton" (CUE). In the autumn of that year, the CUE Board of Governors voted to remove all references to Lutheran and Christian commitment from the mission/vision/values statement. This action was taken with no advance notice to me or any other entity or officer of Lutheran Church–

Canada. In fact, CUE did not even invite any representative of the church to a town-hall meeting convened on its campus toward the end of that year to explain the change.

In fairness, it must be acknowledged that the church and its people had not offered strong levels of financial support to CUE as the years progressed. The surprising election of an NDP provincial government in Alberta in 2015 was cited by some as meaning that it would just be a "matter of time" until Concordia's viability would be threatened if it did not "go public," so to speak. My own sense was that, if anyone could manage that demanding balancing act, Dr. Krispin was that man. It would be difficult to express in few words the bitter disappointment that CUE's action caused, especially because it involved no advance consultation or warning.

Dr. Krispin did agree to make himself available at a public forum for the church held at an Edmonton parish in early 2016. Neither that, nor my own approach to him prior to that gathering, had any effect on the lamentable decision. As one of the consequences of the action initiated under his leadership, he resigned from the clergy roster of the Synod at that time.

To be sure, many honourable Christian people remained on the staff and within the student body of CUE, including several colleagues on the LCC clergy roster. If the founding of Concordia College in 1921 brought pride and joy to our church family in western Canada, its loss from the synodical family 94 years later was a matter of pain and profound sorrow.

LCC Restructuring

In part to answer the concerns of people in the 1980s who were concerned about leaving the Missouri Synod to form a self-governing Lutheran Church–Canada, our Synod fashioned its original Handbook—in other words, its Constitution and Bylaws—after the pattern we knew from Missouri. It did not take long after LCC's 1988 constituting convention for people to sense that our structure was cumbersome, since the Missouri Synod pattern came from a church body many, many times our size.

Unsuccessful attempts to change LCC's structure were made in the 1990s, though some changes were ultimately approved in the early years of the new millennium. By the time I was elected to my third term in 2014, there was a strong sense that the old way was simply not working well and needed to be streamlined.

Various factors contributed to the desire for change: technology which made online meetings and communications possible in a way no one could imagine in 1988; the tendency for local congregations to retain ever more of their offerings at home for parish work so that the level of mission support for the church-at-large decreased; the fading ability of Districts—most notably, the Central District—to maintain the kind of support-system it had offered its parishes in the past; and many more. There is little doubt that, once the CEF crisis took place in the ABC District, many people in that segment of the church and elsewhere were discouraged about our cumbersome way of functioning and wanted something different.

The Commission on Constitutional Matters and Structure (CCMS), under the chairmanship of Rev. William Ney, had primary responsibility to work on this area. By 2015, the CCMS felt that its membership was not sufficiently large to tackle an assignment of this magnitude, so it appointed several non-voting advisory members to expand its ranks. The CCMS also felt ill equipped to have a comprehensive proposal ready in time for the 2017 LCC Convention, since its members all served in their spare time in addition to other ministries and assignments. The Commission therefore engaged an LCC pastor, Rev. Dr. Lester Stahlke of Edmonton, to be its professional consultant for the project. Dr. Stahlke was well known, especially in western Canada, as a long time Executive Director of the Lutheran Association of Missionaries and Pilots (LAMP), and also through the books he had published on the subject of church governance.

From late 2015 to mid-2017, Dr. Stahlke and the CCMS carried out an extensive program involving a national survey, countless interviews, group meetings, and presentations on restructuring. One of the most noticeable proposals involved doing away with the Districts as ecclesiastical arms of the Synod, and to have only one corporate structure headquartered in Winnipeg, functioning under a single (Synodical) Board of Directors. District conventions, budgets, boards, committees, and so forth would be discontinued. Since spiritual supervision would be a challenge in a country as large as Canada, the former District presidents would be replaced by "Regional Pastors" who would provide pastoral and theological support without having to serve as CEOs of separate District corporations. There was considerable discussion about the number and boundaries of the proposed regions, as well as about what nomenclature would be used for the Synod's spiritual leaders.

In the summer of 2017, the CCMS and LCC Board of Directors determined that, although they favoured many of the central proposals of restructuring, they were unwilling to present them under a draft document known as the Act and Bylaws, which was intended to replace the customary LCC Handbook. It was their preference to see the changes enacted instead by means of extensive changes to the existing Statutory Bylaws, Synodical Constitution, and Synodical Bylaws. I fully supported the CCMS and Board of Directors' approach that summer, since I was aware that significant opposition had arisen to the draft document. I shared the concern of many colleagues that insisting on the proposed form could result in the defeat of significant restructuring altogether. Dr. Stahlke concluded his work as restructuring consultant at that point, but I can say without reservation that the subsequent success of the restructuring proposals came about in no small measure due to his tireless work and expert guidance.

Because the restructuring process was so massive, the Board of Directors decided to postpone the Eleventh LCC Convention from June until October, 2017. The Convention, originally planned for Regina, was moved to Kitchener because of the significant cost-savings that venue could offer. The gathering, which happened just two weeks before the 500th Anniversary of Luther's Reformation, convened under the theme "Christ Alone, Christ Forever." Restructuring was obviously the primary focus of the gathering. In the end, the voting delegates gave 76 percent approval to the new Statutory Bylaws, 92 percent to the amended Synodical Constitution, and approval of the Synodical Bylaws took place by a show of hands without dissent. In the required six-month "ratification period" following the Convention, LCC congregations which participated in that phase approved the changes by an overwhelming level of approval.

My own time in the office was drawing to a close. The church was aware that my wife had suffered multiple cancers in 2006 and 2008.

The Lord graciously spared her life, but the side-effects of her cancer treatment had caused other medical difficulties. I felt duty bound to lay aside the work that required extensive travel and absences from home each year, and had advised the Synod in early 2017 that I would not be a candidate for a fourth term. Though I was hopeful God would open a door for me to continue serving, I had no other call at the time of my decision to stand down. Later in 2017, however, I received and accepted a call as pastor to First Lutheran Church and Christian Academy in Windsor, Ontario, with the move to be postponed until after I completed my commitment to the Synod.

The Eleventh Convention elected Rev. Timothy Teuscher of Stratford, Ontario to succeed me and become the fourth President of Lutheran Church–Canada. Rev. Thomas Kruesel of Campbell River, B.C., who had been such an encouragement as one of three vice-presidents during my time, was chosen to be the lone Vice-President under the new structure. My term formally came to an end on January 15, 2018, and I had the honour of installing the new President in a service at Saint James Lutheran Church, Winnipeg, later that month.

Spiritual Challenges Now and for Tomorrow

During LCC's discussions on restructuring, it was said many times that "restructuring alone cannot revitalize the church." One of the strongest voices making that point was Dr. Stahlke himself. Who could possibly disagree? In fact, every time we celebrate the installation of a pastor, we hear the truth again that "God gathers His Church by and around His Holy Gospel and thereby also grants it growth and increase according to His good pleasure."[3]

---

3   *Lutheran Service Book Agenda.* Concordia Publishing House, 2006: 178.

Canada has secularized rapidly during the years since my ordination in 1982. Nor is it just a matter of waning church attendance and other kinds of fading that have happened throughout many Canadian church bodies and congregations. In many ways, the people of our land have become strangers to Jesus and the Good News of His rescue. Even those whose families may have a long history in one of our congregations are not going to remain present and active just because of family heritage, and certainly not because everyone around them is an active Christian. They're not! Nearly all the societal encouragements that smiled on church membership and religious involvement years ago have evaporated.

This does not mean we have to apologize for our faith, or "pack it in" and accept some inevitable decline and death of our congregations. When the psalmist sings, "This is the day the Lord has made, we will rejoice and be glad in it" (118:24), I take him to mean that we ought to embrace the time that God has given to us as a gift. We can fill it with good cheer and hope and prayer, understanding that there are benefits from living and serving Christ in this time that were not always there in an earlier "easier" time.

This moment is going to require God's people to live by Word and prayer, immersing themselves in reading and study of the Scripture, and calling out to Him for help and guidance to meet the challenges we face as individual believers and as a church body. It will require pastors who, like Martin Luther himself, are learned men, but also real God-fearers who pray for those under their care and strive to preach and teach salvation in Jesus in clear language that is faithful to the Bible and also clearly aimed at the needs of the people they serve. It will require congregations that are true "church families," where the saving Gospel of Jesus permeates the worship, and where holy love is the trademark of relationships among the members.

In my estimation, the Lord is actually favouring us by allowing us to live in a time that is closer to the situation faced by the early Christians. In His unshakeable Word and in the holy Sacraments that Jesus has entrusted to us, we have the treasures we need to endure in the confession of Christ to the end. More than that, we have a message to proclaim in our conversations with those around us who do not know Him. And we have Christ's own promise that He will stand with us as long as the world endures.

In other words, the strength of Lutheran Church–Canada— or its weaknesses—will be decided in the local congregations across the country where God has placed us and privileged us to live for Jesus Christ. If the years God gave me to serve the Synod as its President helped to encourage our people in the life they share in those local church families, I will count it as a time of blessing indeed. I sincerely thank the representatives of those churches in Convention who gave me their trust by electing me three times in 2008, 2011, and 2014. And I commend this family of pastors, deacons, and congregations to the care and keeping of the Lord. To Christ be everlasting glory!

THE HISTORY OF FRENCH LANGUAGE MINISTRY IN LUTHERAN CHURCH–CANADA

David H. Somers

T he "French fact" was an oft-mentioned element in discussions leading up to the formation of Lutheran Church–Canada (LCC) in January 1989. While perhaps not a chief concern for all, certainly this reality was not lost on those who were mission minded. It was a uniquely Canadian opportunity, one perhaps better addressed by a Canadian entity, whose territory included six million Francophones—roughly a quarter of the nation's population at the time, and largely unaware of the Lutheran Church and its Gospel message. A look at the map of the distribution of pre-LCC Lutheran Church—Missouri Synod congregations in Canada quickly illustrated the proximity of the challenge and the enormity of the opportunity, too obvious to be brushed aside. The following is a brief history of what has transpired since LCC's undertaking mission work in the French language, preceded by a short summary of prior work by the

LCMS in Canada.[1]

On November 15, 1948, the Ontario District of the LCMS reported correspondence with a student at Concordia Seminary in Saint Louis, Missouri, concerning the possibility of French-language work in Quebec. No mission work resulted from that contact. However, such work did begin in 1965 when the English District of the LCMS sponsored a *Centre de documentation et rencontres* in Montreal, which eventually gave rise to two francophone missions in Montreal. While that full-time French work was being consolidated, similar work was being planned by the Ontario District of the LCMS in West Quebec. The district's official publication, *The Supplement*, confidently declared: "We are ready to begin, for the first time in the nearly 100-year history of the Ontario District, mission work in the French language."

The city of Gatineau was deliberately selected so that the new mission would be surrounded by the care and support of the seven English-language LCMS churches then in the area. That ministry was launched in 1976, backed by simultaneous French work through Our Redeemer (Buckingham, Quebec) and was organized under the name *L'Église évangélique luthérienne du Sauveur Vivant*. Door-to-door surveys, small-group Bible studies, and newspaper announcements conveyed the message that the Lutherans were now present. A fifteen-minute Quebec-produced radio program, *Au pays des vivants*, was broadcast weekly by a private radio network, eliciting much listener response. This program provided another means to heighten awareness of the Lutheran presence and its Bible-based

---

1   A more detailed account is presented in "Lutheran Missionary Activity Among Quebec Francophones in the Late-Twentieth Century." Somers, David. *Historical Papers, 1993: Canadian Society of Church History*, 1993: 247-259.

message. Indeed, the first family of Lutherans-to-be came to the mission through that program. The initial flurry of activity in outreach and response in both Montreal and Gatineau gave rise to great expectations. These two spheres of activity were enthusiastically seen as only small beginnings of bigger things to come.

Lack of growth, however, saw the closing of English District (LCMS) Montreal missions by the 1990s, just after LCC's formation. By then no more than four-score had become Lutheran through any of the French work. *Sauveur Vivant* had seen a period of limited growth through the 1980s. Part of the Gatineau mission strategy had been to build a Lutheran church facility to establish a visible symbol of permanency in the context of strong Roman Catholic institutionalism and cultural considerations, hoping that facility would strengthen outreach efforts. Nevertheless, that congregation too fell prey to the pressures of perceived insufficient response to the outreach and the costs of maintaining an underused building and was closed in 1996. Importantly, however, *Sauveur Vivant* meanwhile did serve as a springboard for expansion of new Montreal work.

In 1990, three disenchanted francophone Pentecostals—of former Roman Catholic background—literally knocked at the door of the English-language Ascension (LCMS) church in Montreal. After having studied the Lutheran Confessions, they had decided they were Lutherans and then sought out the church. The LCMS English congregation was not ready to begin working in French and so the pastor contacted LCC's Missionary-at-large (MAL) in Gatineau. Eventually, in September 1992, their presence gave rise to the founding of a preaching station that became *de l'Ascension* congregation, part of LCC's East District (formerly called the Ontario District).

That start in turn quickly led to the establishment of a mission station in Sherbrooke that became *La Réconciliation* congregation.

By the turn of the twentieth century, clearly the vision of a francophone church made up of French-Canadian former Roman Catholics was not to be. There was no human compulsion to join the Lutheran Church. Many were the reasons in Quebec not to become part of the unknown or oft-maligned Lutheran church; among which were rising secularism, blanket rejection of the Church because of multiple abuses (Roman Catholicism perceived as the only form of Christianity), a presumed necessary denial of French-Canadian identity in adopting "English" Protestantism, weak institutional presence, minuscule adherents with little social commonality cohesion among them.

That failure did not translate into the downfall of the mission, quite the opposite. Obstacles notwithstanding, steady growth had never ceased—ever so slowly, too slowly for the LCMS (English District) to continue work and for LCC to sustain support in Gatineau. Still, one by one people were brought to the church by word of mouth, immigration, and increasingly through internet contact—rarely through the many intentional outreach efforts of the mission. Through whatever means they came, the church responded with the relentless teaching of the Word.

Dashed initial hopes were accompanied by spoken and unspoken reservations about the value and viability of the French ministries. The twentieth-century Canadian experience of gathering Lutherans who quickly organized congregations had been the Ontario District norm. The French ministries, though, were similar to foreign missions and other of LCC's so-called domestic "ethnic ministries" in their need for long-term support that some thought a drain on church finances. The forbearance, persistence, faith, prayer, as well as considerable resources invested were not for naught. Building up Lutheran church culture like that known to the wider church takes generations.

Quite unexpectedly and marvelously, other unimagined avenues for growth opened. Instead of the planned-for source of membership, in the 1990s a new flow of immigrants from Madagascar to French Canada materialized and within a decade there were several hundred Malagasy Lutherans in Quebec. Francophones, they gravitated to the LCC missions even though their mother church body, the *Fiangonana Loterana Malagasy* (FLM), was not in fellowship with LCC.[2] Those Malagasy Lutherans continued the evangelistic activity they had known at home, and brought other Malagasies into LCC. So many were they that, by 2010, FLM congregations were being organized in Montreal, Trois-Rivières, and Quebec City—often including FLM members that had been under LCC care. There were also francophone Protestant African immigrants—mostly Reformed and Lutheran Cameroonians, but also from other central African countries. All were attracted to the Word and Sacrament foundation of LCC and accordingly made professions of faith in our churches.

Increased immigration from Brazil signalled the arrival of a number of Brazilian Lutherans to Quebec, as elsewhere in Canada. Indeed, several pastors from the Evangelical Lutheran Church of Brazil (*Igreja Evangélica Luterana do Brasil* - IELB) have served congregations in LCC. Since its beginning, *de l'Ascension* in Montreal saw Brazilian students attending services while in Montreal for studies, but twenty years later, young families from Brazil began

---

2   The FLM was in fellowship with the Evangelical Lutheran Church in Canada (ELCIC) but that body has no francophone congregations.

to arrive and stay. As they settle in Quebec, some have moved to Quebec City where, as did those in Montreal, they invite their compatriots to be part of the LCC congregations.

The characteristically majority-immigrant make-up of LCC congregations holds true for Sherbrooke, Montreal, and Quebec City. Especially in cosmopolitan Montreal, this pattern is reflected in other Protestant francophone churches. It cannot be missed that this pattern of a recent-immigrant-based membership of the francophone missions uncannily closely resembles the beginnings of Lutheranism in Canada in previous centuries. Other immigrants from Italy, France, and Haiti have also joined the francophone LCC ranks, as did a few LCC anglophones. One major difference: most of these immigrants were not from European Lutheran churches, but rather members of church bodies resulting from mission work: daughter churches in Africa, South America, and Haiti. Another difference, many of the members became Lutheran in Quebec, coming from other churches, sects, and world religions. Yet another distinction is that French, the language of worship of the French ministries, was not the first language of most of the membership yet served as its lingua franca. While immigration bolstered membership, more French-Canadian former Roman Catholics also become Lutheran and constitute roughly one-fifth of those in LCC's French congregations.

Several hundred individuals would be received into membership through the subsequent LCC phase of the French ministries. The student and immigrant-based make-up of the membership was highly mobile, a trait that translated into instability for French congregations, but also the occasion for these new LCC members to become part of LCC elsewhere: in Moncton, New Brunswick; Halifax,

Nova Scotia; and in Ottawa, Ontario. Others returned to their home countries and carried with them their new-found Lutheran faith.

If there was any strategy, it was that of flexibility, spontaneity, and of seizing opportunities as they became apparent. That modus operandi was in step with LCC philosophy for international missions: proclaim the Gospel by any appropriate means. It is important to note that spontaneity did not equal chaos. Mistakes were of course made, but so were wise decisions; trial and error was often the rule, with blessings ultimately outweighing missteps. Missionaries-at-large were expected to be creative in outreach, without increased funding or the security of a permanent location.

A series of subsequent forays, tentative mission plants, led to activities in Montreal's West Island, Granby, Saint-Jean, Saint-Lambert, Trois-Rivières, Quebec City, and in Moncton, New Brunswick. French-language services were also held in Edmonton and Regina. Some of the efforts never took hold, some lasted a while, some rooted and produced fruit. In the case of Quebec City, some members moving there were ready to start services in a home, then a library, and then in a university chapel, before renting a church building. Sometimes, the initial meetings took the form of Vacation Bible Schools or Bible studies; each effort varied according to circumstances. Gone was the luxury of the congregations' use of their own buildings seen in the three LCMS-initiated missions. By 2010, all activities took place in rented or free-of-charge facilities, usually Roman Catholic or Anglican churches, but also occasionally Lutheran (most notably the long-standing rented space at LCMS Ascension in Montreal). In all cases, no building was purchased, no additional administrative structure was created, no committees formed, no personnel were added; a "mobile church" of boxes of hymnals, Bibles, and communion ware were the only material tools.

Another aspect of the French Ministries was the *Centre Vision Chrétienne*, the only francophone and Canadian chapter of the LCMS Lutheran Blind Mission's outreach. The guiding principle was to allow the blind community itself to direct its own activities in a Christian setting, while being assisted by sighted church members only as necessary. Two new blind Lutherans at *de l'Ascension* volunteered to reach out to other visually handicapped members of the wider community to organize a monthly meal, fellowship, and Bible study using a Braille edition of Luther's Small Catechism in French. The group also formed a choir that regularly sang at church events. The death of some members and others moving away brought this endeavour to an end by 2018, after a decade of service.

By the second decade of the twenty-first century, the French ministries continued to grow, adding new members from outside LCC with a relatively younger constituency than elsewhere in the church. Financial independence increased to a level that covers local expenses but not enough for pastoral care, which continued to be largely supported by LCC. The future of the French ministries is precarious as synodical funding falls short and congregational participation, while increasing, is not sufficient to make up the difference. Both locally and externally, concerted efforts are being undertaken to ensure the work continues so as to bestow God's blessings of life and salvation through the work.

The question of pastoral care to carry on the work is perpetual. There again, plans to train church workers to work in French from among the new francophone Lutheran membership were not to be.

Four individuals who were seminary-trained ultimately left the ministry and the Lutheran church; another two enrolled but never began their program. Nevertheless, pastors became available through other means, further underscoring that the ways of God are not the ways of man. An unexpected development was the Canadian Forces' stationing of bilingual LCC military chaplains at Val-Cartier in the Quebec City area just as the mission there was being formed. Their presence covered the first eight years of the new mission in Quebec City, not only providing supply pastors, but also, with their families, members for the new mission, supervised by the East District MAL. The chaplains also held Lutheran services of the Word at the Val-Cartier chapel. That chaplain support was strengthened by a retired pastor who, with his wife, chose to move to Quebec, learn French, and participate in the LCC francophone undertaking. Since inception of that mission, which became *Sainte-Trinité* congregation, he has served as the resident pastoral advisor. In addition, two doctoral students—both Lutheran pastors—one from Haiti and one from Brazil came to Quebec City to study, and officiate as they are able, while employed outside the church.

As French work continued in Canada and Lutheran growth mushroomed in Africa, a pressing need grew for literature to instruct and edify those brought into the francophone churches. The French ministries took on the role of gathering confessional Lutheran documentation and encouraging other organizations to publish more. This increase in production came about through several avenues. The response was heartening. Already, LCC had early established the modest-in-scope French Literature Project to produce materials in partnership with *L'Église évangélique luthérienne - Synode de France et de*

Belgique. Good News magazine as well as the Lutheran Heritage Foundation (LHF) accepted the proposal to furnish materials in French in cooperation with LCC French ministries. The Lutheran Women's Missionary League-Canada (LWMLC) broadened its financial support to include printing of French materials, the French translation of which was done jointly by a team in Montreal and LCC's sister church in France.

By far, the broadest, longest support for outreach materials came from the Lutheran Laymen's League of Canada/Lutheran Hour Ministries-Canada (LLL-C or LHM-C). LLL's significant involvement in French ministry in Canada dated back to the 1970s with a Canadian-produced Lutheran Hour radio program in French (*Au pays des vivants*). When that program was discontinued in the 1980s, LHM continued assisting the French-language mission through radio spot campaigns offering various booklets and occasional special broadcasts for Christmas and Easter. As access to radio and television became increasingly restricted by the media themselves, LLL-C turned to increasing production of Project Connect booklets and making them available online to be accessed not only throughout Canada, but also in France and many countries throughout Africa. Indeed, as they become available, LHM devotionals and booklets are regularly sent to growing numbers of francophone Lutheran bodies in the world, mostly in Africa, but also in Haiti and even to a new LCMS francophone mission in New York City.

The two most significant LCC French ministry contributions on the world level were supported by several sources. The more important is the 2009 LCC French hymnal, *Liturgies et cantiques luthériens,* that has become the standard hymnal for the growing number of Lutheran churches in francophone countries. It is the only French-language Lutheran service book and hymnal available anywhere and is the most comprehensive one ever published. The other is the ever-evolving website that serves as the world's largest gathering point for the rather sparse French-language Lutheran resources, be they liturgical, doctrinal, catechetical, or devotional. The French ministry was also instrumental in the reprinting of the only version of the Book of Concord available in French, coinciding with the 500th anniversary of the Reformation in 2017.

Two events beyond the purview of the church contributed unexpectedly to strengthening the LCC French ministries. First was the 500th anniversary of the Reformation which, through media coverage, afforded heightened awareness of Martin Luther and highlighted the global significance of the Reformation, allowing for appreciation of Lutheranism by the general public. The second event from outside with a major impact inside was COVID-19.

In Quebec, the 500th anniversary sparked an interest that manifested itself in a theretofore unseen level of communication with us from non-Lutheran churches in a swell of ecumenical sentimentalism, individuals and religious institutions seeking materials and explanations about the essence of the Lutheran Reformation. The liturgy periodical of the Canadian Conference of Catholic Bishops requested submission of an article on Luther's liturgical reforms. These contacts allowed for accurate information to be shared through participation in Reformation-themed conferences, an LCC-sponsored year-long series of exhibitions and presentations showcased at the downtown Montreal Bible Society centre, as well as talks, articles, and documentation distribution elsewhere. Still more important, visitors began showing up at services, motivated by curiosity, ecumenical solidarity, and truth-seeking. The Reformation visibility was enhanced by a then recently-revamped and updated website made possible through support from LWMLC and LHM in cooperation with the East District Department for Outreach. Exposure in the francophone Quebec press on the historical and cultural significance of the Reformation further fueled the positive coverage.

Then COVID-19 hit. Safety measures such as physical distancing, protocols, and confinement instituted for the public's well-being motivated the search for creative avenues for the francophone congregations to live as the people of God during the pandemic.

The new norm became frequent calling, texting, mailing, and emailing all members and contacts to reassure, edify, and instruct. The number of worship services, with more historic liturgical diversity, was increased, and a weekly Bible study through Zoom began. Included in the diffusion of information were daily devotions, weekly written Bible studies, and sermons for adults, as well as videos and worksheets on each Sunday's Gospel lesson for children. Work that had to be done was thus delivered through new mediums.

This increased communication in depth and breadth was well-received. Soon, more than ever, families began enrolling their children for online catechetical Christian instruction that necessitated full and active support of their parents at home. Long-absent members began to re-connect and 2020 saw twenty new members added to the missions. Never before were worship services so consistently well-attended. Another key outcome of the COVID-19 situation was the strengthening of ties with *L'Église évangélique luthérienne - Synode de France (ÉÉL-SF)* through online services, Bible studies, and participation in a newly zoom-accessible lay training program.

Zoom also opened the way for another mission foray: a new joint Vespers service with Good Shepherd/*Bon Berger*, Moncton, for the francophones of New Brunswick and elsewhere. When time came for the reopening of churches in Quebec, members began stepping up willingly and enthusiastically in Christian charity, with patience and helpfulness under the health measures protocol—demonstration of an *esprit de corps* at new levels. A French-language LHM C Facebook page was launched in cooperation with LCC and *ÉÉL-SF* to post daily devotionals in French and offer Project Connect booklets (translated in earlier years, but often underread). The response was unprecedented, by far surpassing results from any other outreach activity in the history of the French ministries. There were thousands of responses in the first two months, overwhelmingly from French-Canadians (as had been the case for the 500th anniversary of the Reformation also)— the very group that had so long shunned outreach three decades earlier. Times had changed and some barriers had fallen: the word "Lutheran" was no longer a pariah.

Far from being disabled during the pandemic, proclamation of the Word was not bound, but flourished. "Built on the Rock the Church doth stand"—even when church buildings are closed, even when congregations cannot meet and commune as before, even when they cannot sing together, they nevertheless can worship as surely as ever.

So now the church is being strengthened, if challenged, and can faithfully preach the Word and administer the Sacrament in new circumstances. We are not paralyzed by new constraints but energized by them. The Gospel is no less effective, no less pro-claimed in these times. Indeed, it is proclaimed all the more, to feed and edify by that abiding Word in times of trouble—a bulwark in the storm. We are not frozen in grief over the paradigm of how things used to be but, instead, pushed to the limits to joyfully, creatively, and fully be led forward in faith to the glory of God. The Church does not know what tomorrow will bring, but certainly knows how to live today: as it always has.

By the grace of God—ever-open to the moving of the Spirit through Word and Sacrament—the LCC French ministries will be led to believe, teach, and confess the faith, by any appropriate means.

ABOUT THE CONTRIBUTORS

Rev. Dr. Norman J. Threinen

Rev. Dr. Norman J. Threinen was born on May 8, 1936 in rural Manitoba and grew up thirteen miles away in rural Saskatchewan. He prepared for the Lutheran ministry in Concordia College (Edmonton) and Concordia Seminary (St. Louis, Missouri), graduating in 1961.

Graduate studies at the St. Louis Seminary earned him a Master of Sacred Theology in 1962 and a Doctor of Theology in 1980. He served the Lutheran Church as a parish pastor at St. Peter's Lutheran Church in Edmonton (1962-1971), a church administrator with the Lutheran Council in Canada (1971-1984), and as a seminary professor at Concordia Lutheran Seminary in Edmonton (1984-2002).

He has researched and written broadly in the area of Canadian Lutheranism. In his latest book, entitled *Landestreu: An Odyssey*, he traced the movement of a Lutheran family from South Germany in the 18th century to present-day Ukraine and thence to Western Canada at the end of the 19th century.

Dr. Threinen has travelled widely and taught at various seminaries in Canada, Ukraine, and Southeast Asia. He lives with his wife Muriel in retirement in Penticton, B.C. They have two grown children: David in Hamilton, Ontario and Deborah in Summerland, B.C.

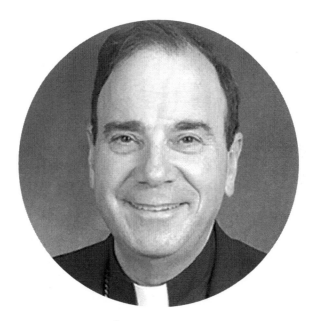

Rev. Dr. Robert Bugbee

Rev. Dr. Robert Bugbee was born in Ohio in 1955, the son of Charles and Violet (Stratton) Bugbee. Baptized and confirmed at

Reformation Lutheran Church (LCA) in Toledo, he retained active membership there until his transfer to The Lutheran Church—Missouri Synod in 1974 for doctrinal reasons.

He earned the Bachelor of Arts in German language and literature from Wartburg College (Waverly, Iowa) in 1977. One year of undergraduate studies took him to the University of Bonn, Germany. He later studied at Concordia Seminary (St. Louis, Missouri) which awarded him the Master of Divinity degree in 1981. During his seminary career he spent two semesters at the Lutheran Theological Seminary (Oberursel, Germany). In May 2010, Concordia Theological Seminary in Fort Wayne, Indiana, conferred on him the honorary degree of Doctor of Divinity.

After graduating from seminary, he was ordained and installed as pastor of Our Saviour Lutheran Church (London, Ontario). He subsequently served parishes in St. Catharines, Ontario, and Albertville, Minnesota, before moving as Senior Pastor to Holy Cross Lutheran Church (Kitchener, Ontario) where he served more than 14 years. He became a proud and grateful Canadian citizen in 2001.

The Eighth Convention of Lutheran Church–Canada elected Rev. Bugbee as Synod President in June 2008, to succeed the retiring Dr. Ralph Mayan. He was re-elected in 2011 and 2014. After declining to stand for a fourth term, he accepted a call as Pastor to First Lutheran Church and Christian Academy in Windsor, Ontario, where he has served since 2018.

He continues to serve on the Board of Directors of the International Lutheran Council, as well as on the three-person ILC Executive Leadership Group. He is also under appointment by

LCC President Timothy Teuscher to represent LCC on dialogue groups with the North American Lutheran Church (NALC) and the Anglican Church in North America (ACNA).

Rev. Bugbee has been married to Gail D. Longaven since 1981. A gracious God blessed their union with four children, now all grown, and seven grandchildren. Rev. Dr. Robert and Gail make their home in LaSalle, Ontario.

Rev. Dr. Edwin Lehman

Rev. Dr. Edwin Lehman was born in Edmonton, Alberta in 1932, the fourth child of Adolph and Wanda Lehman, who had emigrated from Poland just a few years earlier. He was baptized in St. Peter's Lutheran Church in Edmonton, and confirmed at Christ Lutheran Church in Mellowdale, Alberta, the family having purchased a farm in that area. After completing grade nine in a one-room school, he enrolled in the high school department of Concordia College, Edmonton, since there was no high school in the rural area in which his family lived. By the time he returned for his second year, God had led him to enroll in the college's ministerial program.

In 1951 he transferred to Concordia Seminary (St. Louis, Missouri), graduating with the degree of Master of Divinity. His vicarage was at St. Paul's Lutheran Church, the mother church in Ottawa, Ontario. In 1987, his alma mater in St. Louis awarded him the honorary Doctor of Divinity degree.

He began his ministry in a four-point parish in east-central Saskatchewan, serving congregations in the Margo, Nut Mountain, and Wadena areas. This was followed by a three-point parish in the central Alberta areas of Red Deer, Craig, and Alhambra. His final years of parish ministry were at Richmond and Ladner, British Columbia. In 1978 he was elected as full-time president of the Alberta-British Columbia District of The Lutheran Church—Missouri Synod.

At the constituting convention of the autonomous Lutheran Church–Canada in May 1988, he was elected president of the new synod, continuing in that office until retiring in 1996. During that time, he also served as chairman of the International Lutheran Council from 1989-1995, and as editor of the ILC News until 1999.

Upon retiring in Edmonton, he was instrumental in establishing the Concordia Lutheran Mission Society, which has since been granted auxiliary organization status in the synod. Also, Dr. L. Dean Hempelmann, then president of Concordia Lutheran Seminary in Edmonton, invited him to head up the Missionary Study Centre at the seminary. He also served as the seminary's acting president for seven months.

In 1956, he married Marge Huber, whom he met while both attended Concordia College. Over the following years, God entrusted them with three children and five grandchildren. In 2015, after a richly blessed marriage of nearly 59 years, Marge was called to her heavenly home.

Rev. Dr. Ralph Mayan

Rev. Dr. Ralph Mayan was born in Yorkton, Saskatchewan on June 25, 1944, the son of Rev. Ernest and Mary Mayan. He attended elementary and high school in Vernon, British Columbia. He graduated from Concordia Seminary (St. Louis, Missouri) with a Master of Divinity in 1971.

As parish pastor Mayan served Zion Lutheran Church (Yorkton, Saskatchewan) and St. Paul Lutheran Church (Springside, Saskatchewan) from 1971-1978. Rev. Mayan then received a divine call to Trinity Lutheran Church of Richmond, B.C. serving that congregation from 1979-1996.

In 1996, Mayan was elected as the second president of Lutheran Church–Canada, holding that position until his retirement in 2008. From 2008-2010 he served as the Interim Mission Executive for Lutheran Church–Canada. He also served as chairman of the International Lutheran Council for eight years.

In 2002, Mayan was awarded an honorary Doctor of Divinity from Concordia Lutheran Seminary in Edmonton.

Rev. Dr. Mayan is married to Linda. Together they have four children and fourteen grandchildren.

Rev. Dr. David H. Somers

Rev. Dr. David H. Somers was born on October 29, 1956 in Reading, Pennsylvania. He received his Bachelor of Arts in French

Studies and Latin American Literature from Indiana University. Continuing his studies at Indiana University he received a Master of Science in Applied Linguistics. His theological training included a Master of Divinity from Concordia Theological Seminary (Fort Wayne, Indiana), as well as a Master of Science in Religious Studies and PhD in Religious Studies from the University of Ottawa.

Somers served for a time with the U.S. Peace Corps as professor at *l'École Normale Supérieure* in Bamako, Mali. He worked from 1984-1987 as Coordinator of the Kalanga Bible Translation Project with The Lutheran Church—Missouri Synod. In 1987, he was called to be Missionary-at-Large for French Ministries in Canada, serving also as vacancy pastor (1988-1991) for the Hispanic Mission of St. Luke's Lutheran Church of Ottawa, Ontario.

Rev. Dr. Somers has been a member of Lutheran Church–Canada's Committee for Mission and Social Ministry Services since 1989. Since 2000, he has also served as a professor for the seminary and continuing education programs of the Lutheran Church Synod of Nicaragua. Dr. Somers is editor of Lutheran Church–Canada's French Hymnal *Liturgies et cantiques luthériens*.

***

Missouri North was edited by Rev. Mark Lobitz, with assistance from Mathew Block. Layout and design are by Alex Steinke.

FURTHER READING

Herzer, John E. *Homesteading for God: A Story of the Lutheran Church (Missouri Synod) in Alberta and British Columbia 1894-1946.* Edmonton, 1946.

Nelson, E. Clifford, ed. *The Lutherans in North America.* Fortress Press, 1980.

Schwermann, Albert H. *The Beginnings of Lutheran Church–Canada.* Edmonton: Lutheran Church–Canada, 1969.

Threinen, Norman J. *A Sower Went Out: A History the Manitoba and Saskatchewan District of Lutheran Church–Canada (Missouri Synod).* Regina: Manitoba and Saskatchewan District, 1982.

Threinen, Norman J. *Fifty Years of Lutheran Convergence: The Canadian Case-Study.* Dubuque, Iowa: Wm. C. Brown Company. Lutheran Historical Conference, 1983.

Threinen, Norman J. *Like a Mustard Seed: A Centennial History of the Ontario District.* Kitchener: Ontario District, 1989.

Threinen, Norman J. *Like a Leaven-A History of the Alberta-British Columbia District Lutheran Church–Canada.* Edmonton: Alberta British Columbia District, 1994.

Threinen, Norman J. *A Sower Went Out: Supplement Covering 1982-1997.* Regina: Central District, 1997.

Threinen, Norman J. *They Called Him Red: The Life and Times of Albert Schwermann.* De Winton, Alberta: Today's Reformation Press, 2008.

Threinen, Norman J. *A Religious-Cultural Mosaic: A History of Lutherans in Canada.* Vulcan, Alberta: Today's Reformation Press 2006.

Threinen, Norman J. *Landestreu, An Odyssey: The Story of a Family Over Time*, Victoria: Friesen Press, 2017.

Wiegner, Paul. *The Origin and Development of the Manitoba-Saskatchewan District of The Lutheran Church—Missouri Synod.* Bruno, Saskatchewan: Manitoba-Saskatchewan District, 1957.

ON THE COVER

Cover design by Alex Steinke, Lutheran Church–Canada's Director of Communications 2022. The cover features artwork (LCC Badge) by Harrison Avery Prozenko, a member of St. Andrew's Lutheran Church of Atlantic Canada in Halifax. Special thanks to Peter Steinke for his assistance with photo editing for *Missouri North*.

Top Left: Travelling to LCC F's Founding Convention in 1958: Rev. Carl Baase, William Fromson, and Rev. Albert Schwermann.

Top Right: Marconi School 1914 Church Attendance. Worship services were held at Marconi School until St. Peter was built (dedicated in May 1921). Photo courtesy of Marilyn Schultz.

Second Row, Left: Concordia College Edmonton, early 1920s.

Second Row, Right: Confirmation at St. Peter (Oxbow, SK) mid-1930s with Pastor Wirth. Photo courtesy of Marilyn Schultz.

Third Row, Left: LCC Founding Convention 1988.

Third Row, Right: Photo taken in Flaxton, North Dakota in 1919 as plans were being made for a new rural congregation South of Oxbow, Saskatchewan (which would become St. Peter Lutheran Church). Pastor Krieger (seated); Bert Loppe; Wilhelm (William) Schendel; Albert Erdman; and Jullius Ludke. Photo courtesy of Marilyn Schultz.

Bottom Row, Left: Ukraine Missionaries circa 1992. Featuring Rev. Roland Syens; Rev. Keith and Barb Haberstock; Irena Sharshakova, Translator; and LCC Director of World Missions, Rev. Dr. Leonard Harms.

Bottom Row, Right: Pages and Helpers at Convention in 1990.

Manufactured by Amazon.ca
Bolton, ON

34578806R00144